T0301119

Mindset
to startup

The mindset and tools you need
to create a value centric business

Hani W. Naguib

B/SPUBLISHERS

BIS Publishers
Borneostraat 80-A
1094 CP Amsterdam
The Netherlands
T +31 (0)20 515 02 30
bis@bispublishers.com
www.bispublishers.com

ISBN 978 90 636 9714 3

Written in Cairo, Egypt.

Book designed by Habiba Abdalla.
Book edited by Melissa Mitchell.

This book is dedicated to Egyptian entrepreneurs.

You imagine, create & implement, armed with almost nothing.

You inspire!

Table of Contents

PART 1 - THE MINDSET JOURNEY

Chapter 3 – The Mindset Journey

Chapter 4 – The Cycles Of Learning

Chapter 5 – The Invisible Power Of Perception

Chapter 6 – The Mindset Journey Kit

1 The Mindset Journey

2 The Startup Journey

The Braided Journey **3**

Inspiration Behind This Book

This book would not have been possible without the lessons I gathered in the field while working with entrepreneurs. Throughout my journey of mentoring these exceptional characters, I've come to see several threads that I believe are commonplace on the journey of all entrepreneurs all across the globe.

I've accompanied countless entrepreneurs all the way from the infancy of their startups to the stages of startup growth activities. I was fascinated, to say the least, by how starting up had a very similar impact on people from different cultures, backgrounds, ages, and experiences. The more I interacted with entrepreneurs, the more I saw that entrepreneurship is about the human experience; not the funds raised or the number of customers acquired.

Yes, it is the human element that is the secret ingredient in any startup; not the technology or the raised funds.

Moreover, the beauty of entrepreneurship is not in all the glamour that comes with success. The beauty of entrepreneurship lies in witnessing those determined spirits, who wake up every day to multiple rejections and, yet, still focus on "failing" forward. It is in the unwavering sense of faith in the intangible, which many entrepreneurs harness to fuel their daily battles with uncertainty.

This is the human experience at the center of the entrepreneurial path and it is one that I have witnessed for a decade.

In this book, I reflect on that decade in the hopes of highlighting the primarily shadowed and unspoken parts of the journey that go far deeper than the hype of unicorns and beyond the glitz of sponsored startups. These amazing and fulfilling experiences offered me a special window into how founders perceive, think, and act in real life!

And so, after a decade of work, I finally decided to sit down, open my notes, and attempt to make sense of it all. The result is what you hold in your hand. My aim isn't just to create a sincere guide to accompany anyone who has decided to build a startup. It is also to share the thrilling stories of all the nameless, faceless, unsung heroes who, despite all the challenges, never stopped dreaming and building something extraordinary.

So, this is my ode – or perhaps, my homage – to you brave souls.

Dear entrepreneurs,

If some of you feel that you have learned something from me, I would like to tell you that, in fact, it was me who has been humbled and taken to school by all of you.

Now, it is my turn to give something back; to describe and share everything I have learned during this decade-long journey and offer it to future entrepreneurs.

As always,
Goodwill and Respect

Hani W. Naguib

"

How will you go
about finding
that thing, the
nature of which
is totally
unknown to you?!

Meno, Greek philosopher

Introduction

We are all entrepreneurs in one way or another. That is because the definition of what it means to be an entrepreneur correlates with the natural curiosity of the human spirit. It is in our essence to ask questions, imagine, and create. Take a look at children in the park and you will find them creating games out of thin air. You'll see them conjuring up big adventures inside their little minds, but you'll also witness them falling and getting up repeatedly – continuing their contribution to their little experience almost completely undeterred. Look at children in schools or try to remember your own childhood. In a classroom, children ask questions, tell stories, color outside the lines, and create beautiful things out of their imaginative minds. They have the propensity to take elementary materials in arts and crafts classes and turn them into the most astounding little pieces of art you've ever seen.

And they get a little bit better every day because they *learn by doing.*

Getting up after falling and learning by doing are two of the most important skills any entrepreneur should possess. But dreaming, which is perhaps the most underrated entrepreneurial quality, is critical too. Dreaming provides the motivation and desire to learn and keep getting up time and time again. We all face the world with our dreams, skills, and motivations, but let us not delude ourselves. Entrepreneurship is not a romantic dream or a Hollywood movie where the hero gets the girl at the end. There are no guarantees in entrepreneurship – not even if you put in the hard work. I have witnessed the shadow of big plans broken on the rocks of reality many times. There is what you have and what you can make out of it. Some, for instance, have determination, grief, loneliness, as well as – of course – money, time, and effort.

Nonetheless, this extraordinary journey of building something is usually stimulated by our environment. We start to look at things with a little bit of defiance to the status quo and consider the long-ignored "what if?"

What if I can make this product cheaper?

What if I can use this technology to make this solution more accessible or faster (or a combination of both)?

What if I can find a better way to deliver this service?

Those questions are the initial sparks that make the world around you glitter with possibilities and potential. How many of you can say that you've experienced that priceless moment – your "start" moment? If you haven't yet, know this: it can come at any time. It has no age requirements and is not restricted to aha moments that come as a result of meditating in a temple on top of a mountain either. It can happen while you are in the shower, running in the park, having coffee with friends, in the middle of a conversation at work, or even while you are sitting and doing absolutely nothing at home.

I'll reiterate. The spirit of entrepreneurship resides deep inside all of us. It may be dormant but it is there; waiting for the right stimulus, experience, or trigger to rise, inspire, and create. It is like all those apps on your smartphone that you never use. Those apps are there. They're unused, perhaps, but they are there; waiting for the right motivation that will push you to tap on the app icon and start using them.

As you'll soon come to learn, ***entrepreneurship is a journey!***

Making The Most Out Of The Book

In this book, I make an attempt to describe what I have witnessed in the field. I use it to put systems of progress into a tangible framework that can be easily used and practiced by founders. In fact, they can be used by just about anyone with a desire to start a business and make progress on their journey.

The purpose of embarking on the journey of entrepreneurship is to build a successful value-focused and evidence-based venture. This is precisely why I offer founders a step-by-step approach to understanding what that could look like.

The book is divided into three main parts aside from the introduction. The first part is dedicated to understanding the ***mindset journey*** and its context. It proposes a framework for its system of progress.

The second part is dedicated to understanding the ***startup journey***. It challenges some common concepts that are often taken for granted and uses an evidence-based approach[1] behind lean startup[2] to materialize a system of progress. This is a system that founders can use and apply in real life.

Finally, the last part is dedicated to proposing a clear interpretation of the ***braided journey*** - a combination of the mindset and startup journey. Here, we'll explore how each system of progress affects the the other and creates a medium for the other.

---

1   This approach to entrepreneurship requires that founders systematically accumulate and interpret evidence of the validity of their ideas.

2   This is a scientific approach to building and managing startups that allows entrepreneurs to move from ideation to iteration faster than normal.

I use many real-life cases from the field as examples to clarify the approach and make some of the concepts introduced in this book tangible. The book is written as a conversation between you – the readers – and in that case, you, as my readers, are potential and existing founders.

However, if you're a mentor, you will find this book equally valuable as there are some nuggets of information peppered throughout this book for you.

Ultimately, this book is my humble attempt to help founders get the best possible outcomes for their journey, to emphasize the importance of the journey over the destination, and to make sure that entrepreneurship is seen as a human endeavor.

This endeavor, at the end of the day, is rooted in the desire to create value and meet worldly challenges with profitable solutions. This book is dedicated to sharing everything I learned from the field, working with entrepreneurs on both the business and the mindset, and how to create progress on both fronts.

So, let's take the first step on your journey.

Mind
set
to startup

The mindset and tools
you need to create a value
centric business

"

**Exploring
the unknown
requires
tolerating
uncertainty**

Brian Greene

01
The Uncertain Journey Of Entrepreneurship

In the Introduction, I mentioned that the spirit of entrepreneurship lies in each one of us but that it might be dormant.

As we unpack the uncertain journey of entrepreneurship, it's important to ask the right questions – starting with "why is it dormant?"

It seems that as we grow up, we get too busy to ask questions. Somewhere along the way, we lose the level of resilience we had in childhood and become too afraid to fall down. Consequently, we stop imagining and creating. In simpler terms, we stop coloring outside the lines. Somehow, we are encouraged to stay within the confines of those lines and miss the entire point of life: that we can create our own lines altogether. Entrepreneurs are silly enough to color outside the lines, brave enough to imagine changing those lines, and hungry enough to actually attempt to do it.

And perhaps that is the most important second moment in the journey of entrepreneurship – when you actually decide to make an idea tangible.

But countless people who dare to dream end up suppressing those dreams out of that same fear of failure.

I'm here to confirm that the journey of entrepreneurship is not about winning or losing. *It is not about success or failure.*

It is more about **progress irrespective of winning and in spite of losing.** Moreover, it's about so much more than the figures on the bottom line at the end of the year.

More Than The Money

For some reason, entrepreneurship has increasingly been perceived as a binary approach to selling products instead of the profound experience behind the journey to create value. It is not enough that a startup can simply reflect a person's dream, solve problems, and make money. Instead, it became this urge to reap unsustainable growth in the now, no matter the consequences later. This stance of doing whatever is needed to reach a glorious initial public offering (IPO) with an unrealistic valuation and a balance sheet in the red is what makes the journey unrealistic and cumbersome.

But the other end of the romanticized spectrum isn't any better because entrepreneurship is not about changing the world as some might lead you to believe. I found that it has more to do with changing lives – starting with the lives of entrepreneurs themselves – and that should be celebrated as well. Anyone who decides to start their own business and works hard to succeed is an entrepreneur. That is no small feat and it shouldn't be treated as such. However, the road ahead depends on the type of person behind the entrepreneurial mask and how far their business can progress.

Let me give you an example from the world of football, or soccer as they call it in some parts of the world.

Some players possess the skills and the drive that win them a spot on the bench of a local league. Others can go on to become key players in some of the world's best teams. The difference between these two groups is only in the players' respective abilities to learn and apply those learnings under pressure in order to make progress. Of course, there is the invisible hand of luck that puts the right people in the right place, sets the right circumstances, and offers rare opportunities on the journey to build and create.

As members of the supporting community of entrepreneurs, we should take the time to dive deeper and reconsider what we have taken for granted. Entrepreneurs are not rock stars. Raising funds is not equivalent to earning a platinum record for selling a million copies of a released hit. Raising funds is equivalent to signing a deal to record a couple of new albums. The point is this: it doesn't guarantee success. It only reflects the confidence in the potential of the "signed group" or, in this case, the entrepreneur.

But the true measure of success is the outcome, not the output. A band can produce many albums to satisfy their contracts. However, if these albums don't make any sense or difference to the listeners, they will respond in kind to the band and not show up for their concerts or buy their records. The outcome will, hence, be reflected in continual poor sales.

I have witnessed many of these cases where entrepreneurs have fallen into the trap of focusing on outputs to please investors. But I have also witnessed those who, despite not having much, were unshakably focused on delivering outcomes to customers. But for that, they had to develop as leaders in their teams. They had to become a source of inspiration to their investors and a beacon that those same investors could follow or believe in.

When I work with startups and founders, my focus has always ranged from ideas to the early stages of the journey. I assisted entrepreneurs in focusing their ideas of value from abstraction to conceptual and, eventually, to tangible. Watching this progress was a great learning experience. It allowed me the rare opportunity to see mindsets evolving, thinking patterns progressing, and interactions moving from merely responding to developing and deploying pre-prepared actions.

That is the key concept here: ***preparation.***

The Walk

Have you ever seen the movie The Walk [1]? It is based on the real story of a 24-year-old French high-wire artist who willingly crossed the space between the two towers of the World Trade Center in the 1970s. He only had a really long bar, known as a balance bar, to help him maintain his balance while attempting to cross over a space that was over 40 meters wide while precariously perched on a wire 500 meters above the ground. To heighten the suspense in this whole situation, he did so with neither a harness nor a safety net beneath him. It was a breathtaking scene, I must admit. The journey to accomplishing this goal was perhaps even more spectacular than that final scene, in which he crossed from one tower to another multiple times.

Now, close your eyes and imagine yourself standing at the edge of this tower. Let's hypothesize for a moment that you have a mentor and that you have followed their guidance to the letter. You've made your calculations as best as possible and, now, you're ready to walk. Now, let's align this with the precarious balancing act that you will commit to as an entrepreneur. Alongside your team, who already feel like brothers at arms more than employees, you have put together the wiring mechanism and pulled the wire from one tower to the other. As these thoughts cross your mind at the speed of light, you consider taking that first step. First, you calculate the wind's speed and direction while pulling that long balancing bar up. You take your first step and move forward one step at a time.

Can you feel the cold air brushing your skin?

Can you sense the beads of sweat beginning to form on your brow?

Do you feel that rush mixed with fear shooting through your whole body at the same time?

Now, imagine that you've reached the halfway point. You've made so much progress, but you're nowhere near the end. At this point, as you stand equidistance away from both towers, there is a sense of no turning back, but the bar starts to feel heavier. The wind feels faster and the wire vibrates beneath your feet. You take a quick look below and, perhaps, for the first time, you can make sense of what 500 meters feels like. You take another step and continue to walk until you have almost reached the other side of the wire. As you are about to take that final step and get to the ledge, you see the police rushing towards you. These obstacles on your journey are there to test you and you freeze for a moment; not knowing what to do next. Then it hits you. This is not the end of the journey. You must go back! So you swiftly and precisely do the unthinkable. You make a 180-degree turn and start walking back to the other tower. You see the police on the other end waiting for you as you reach halfway. Suddenly, the wire feels like the only safe place on the journey. So you continue taking one step after another with a slight hint of familiarity. You keep telling yourself, I have been here before and can do it again. But then the rushing wind blows off that sense of familiarity as you struggle to use the balancing bar to keep yourself from falling. You regain your balance, pause for a moment, and carefully take another step towards the ledge of the other tower. As the police officers approach it, you stop and decide to go back.

Now, open your eyes.

How uncertain was that journey?

Truth be told, as soon as you left that ledge, you were stepping into the unknown, testing the unfamiliar, and balancing the unpredictable. You can't go back to where you first started or finish it until you have accomplished what you need to. Now, imagine attempting to make that walk from one tower to the other without much training or practice. Add to this the fact that you've never been up that high and on top of that, you have a moderate fear of heights.

That is entrepreneurship in a nutshell.

Entrepreneurship is the journey of making progress despite limited resources in the face of pressure-filled uncertainty with continuous learning. There will be many turning points when it feels like you're doubling back on yourself and many obstacles that make you feel like you're falling right before you reach the finish line. At the end of the day, the journey consists of two main fronts: the mindset journey and the startup or business journey. They both feed on each other and act as a medium to help the other propagate and expand. Both are so intertwined that they usually seem and feel like one huge thing. But I can tell you, as a mentor with a decade of experience in accompanying entrepreneurs on their high-rope act, that both exist distinctly. Additionally, both affect each other tremendously in both a positive and negative light.

My Uncertain Journey

The Setting

In 2010, I had just finished my MBA in Italy and headed back home to Cairo, Egypt. I remember the date – the 22nd of December, 2010. I was starting a new job at my old firm with an excellent promotion to Vice President of Business Development, responsible for all of the firm's Western European clients. After a short rest, I started my new job – that was on the 8th of January, 2011. Everything was going well with my new role and I had huge plans that I was incredibly eager to implement. With the support of management, I started the implementation right away.

On the 25th of January, 2011, a group of young people went to Tahrir Square and voiced their requests for change. It was not taken seriously. But everything changed on Friday the 28th when that peaceful protest turned into violence. All that we had known and took for granted was suddenly non-existent. It was the beginning of the Arab Spring in Egypt.

The Preparation Phase

At that time, work had understandably reached a standstill. There were no projects or clients and we could not anticipate how matters would go with any certainty. Our offices were very hard to get to because of all of the demonstrations paired with the resulting violence on the next streets. Management, therefore, quickly decided that we could work from home until things calmed down. With all the free time on my hands, I turned to my favorite escape: reading. I had a big pile of books that I had collected during my MBA – books that I had never gotten around to reading. One book led to another, and one topic to another.

Like many of my fellow countrymen, I thought about what I could do to help during this time of need and what I could do to pitch in. Around me, many people joined political parties and either established or joined charity foundations as well as social development NGOs. But for some reason, these options didn't feel like something that aligned with me.

Fast forward to the summer of 2012 and I found myself sitting with some friends, discussing current events and the news. Everyone was sharing their projections of the future, but I noticed that one friend was sitting unusually silent. I turned to him and asked him if everything was alright. He had started his own business in the fall of 2010 and as we started chatting about this venture further, he revealed a number of fears and hangups. I guided him to see potential alternatives for his business and I believe that was my very first mentoring session.

As uncertainty increased with the events unfolding all around us, **my time was divided into three main areas:**

- Reading and learning
- Meeting people with struggling businesses to help them find alternatives
- Following up on the news.

The days went by so fast that I really didn't realize it. One might say, I blinked and all of a sudden it was 2014.

The Start Moment

I spent those two years learning and implementing what I learned in the field as well as interacting with struggling business owners. One June morning, I was sitting with a business owner and sharing the insights and tools that I collected from my sessions. After a while, he looked at me and asked me whether we could work together on his business model. He wanted to try to find a way to make it more adaptable to the current business environment. We met almost every evening for a couple of hours over the next couple of weeks. We mapped out the business environment and developed an ambitious strategy to compete and adapt. But the significant event came in the form of something he said to me. He said that, for the first time since the revolution started, he felt equipped with the tools and mindset to help him respond to what happens to his business. He felt empowered.

It was as if a glowing light bulb went on above my head at that moment. I thought, 'What if I can do the same for more people?'
What if I can empower and help more people by sharing everything I learned and practiced through merging design thinking, lean startup, and visual working together?

That day, I decided to quit my job at the firm and put everything I learned into one slide deck. And that was my "Start!" moment. It also, amazingly, became the answer to my earlier question of what I could do to help and contribute.

The Next Phase

Throughout my journey, I have worked with more than one thousand entrepreneurs as a mentor, offering more than ten thousand volunteered hours of one-on-one mentorship for early- stage founders. I've worked on developing tools and approaches to assist founders with their value-focused, evidence-based approaches. These tools are in the mindset and startup journey kit chapters and this is precisely why it's imperative for you to know how these tools came to be.

These are not random opinions or tools based on loose, second-hand research. These are factual and practical elements that have come about through hands-on experience. But before you can move on and begin exploring these tools, here is what I took away as the key insights of my mentoring sessions.

66

The intangible
represents
the real power
of the universe.
It is the seed
of the tangible.

Bruce Lee

02
The Key Insights of The Mentoring Sessions

In my mentoring sessions, I never gave entrepreneurs proverbial fish. My aim was to teach them how to fish. The focus of all my sessions was to help them see the blind spots in their startup logic and not to offer them opinions of my own. As I often observed, that logic was definitely impacted by the person's psychological state at the time and that is why I started to give attention to the mindset of the human being behind the entrepreneur. I provided the entrepreneur with a safe space to explore thoughts and associated feelings. I was curious about the impact of that exploration on the entrepreneur's performance at the startup level. So, my mentoring had to include both sides of the equation to achieve results.

After a decade of mentoring sessions with entrepreneurs from different backgrounds, ages, genders, and experiences, some patterns began to emerge. In this coming section, I will share with you the insights that I collected. These were collated via a Google form that I would give entrepreneurs to fill out when they requested a mentoring session. These questions were created to help me prepare for the mentoring session and this data would be combined with the notes taken accumulatively during all my sessions.

Let's dive into the insights with Key Insight #1.

Key Insight 1

40%

OF THE ENTREPRENEURS REQUESTING A MENTORING SESSION THOUGHT THEIR STARTUP WAS AT THE PRODUCT- MARKET FIT PHASE.

After my first meeting with these entrepreneurs, I found these repeating observations:

1. Most entrepreneurs were, in fact, not in product-market fit testing but rather in problem-solution fit finding. They just did not know the difference.

2. Most entrepreneurs did not have a clear value proposition (solution) and mainly showcased features (solution components). When I asked them how these features would fix the problem, I usually got ambiguous answers about selling the solution. The problem was not well defined.

3. Most entrepreneurs saw product-market fit as a sales and advertising activity and did not include the competition or the customer in the equation. They did not have a strategy; only a product that they hoped to push on customers with growth-hacking sales techniques when they raised enough funds from investors.

> What we can take from this is that many entrepreneurs are fixated on providing investors with the right answers, even if it means ignoring the exploration and understanding of customer value. Furthermore, many think that investor money is the only missing ingredient in their startup recipe. What many discover later on is that they don't have a startup worth investing in because it doesn't offer any real customer value.

Key Insight 2

20%

OF THE ENTREPRENEURS REQUESTING MENTORING SESSIONS HAD A WORKING PRODUCT PROTOTYPE BUT DIDN'T KNOW WHAT TO DO NEXT.

When examining the issue with them, we discovered the following common reasons for this:

1. They finished the prototype without any contact or actual interaction with potential customers. In other words, they had a finished product with zero customer validation.

2. They were more focused on building the perfect product from their own point of view and requested the session to get a confirmation of their own point of view.

3. The relatively young founders dealt with the product with the same mentality they used to deal with their undergrad graduation projects at university: as a means to an end. They wanted to finish the best product possible (project) to get the best possible funding (grade).

> The key takeaways here are that many founders get fixated on developing wonderful tech that they think is perfect. They compromise everything for the sake of building the perfect tech. As many of them learn later on, a startup can launch with a less-than-perfect product as long as it can materialize true value from the customers' perspective. They also learn the hard way that investors are not keen on offering them a research grant to develop the perfect tech. Investors put money in products that can offer enough value that customers would be happily willing to pay for and, thus, create value for the business.

Key Insight 3

~25%

OF ENTREPRENEURS WERE JUST SEEKING IDEA CONFIRMATION.

The sessions had these common repeating traits:

1. The sessions always started with a bombardment of yes or no questions. The entrepreneurs were always eager to get specific answers out of me. It felt more like a negotiation where the entrepreneurs were trying to reassure themselves of the success of their ideas.

2. In many cases, entrepreneurs sought to respond to negative comments from investors and other well-known "ecosystem" individuals. They were primarily looking for a validated response to "the criticism." Some even asked me if they could quote me directly on the validity of their idea to use in discussions with potential investors.

3. Most of these sessions were what I like to call a "one- timer." They come for confirmation and never show up again when they see the blindspots in their startup logic of value. It is understandable. Seeing the flaws meant that the startup might not take off, and they could not have that. So, instead of the opinion-based validation, they got confirmation on "the criticism."

4. For a few of them, the session was an eye-opener. It motivated them to consider seeing the startup from a perspective different from theirs – the customer's perspective – using field validation activities.

This is a very interesting insight because it shows how much the opinion of a founder can stand in the way of the startup progress. By fixating on the opinion of mentors and investors, founders dilute their perspective to an extent that stands in the way of their own original thinking.

Key Insight 4

45%

OF THE ENTREPRENEURS REQUESTING A MENTORING SESSION INDICATED THAT THEY HAD REACHED THE PROBLEM-SOLUTION FIT PHASE AND THAT CUSTOMERS DIDN'T APPRECIATE THE VALUE THEY WERE OFFERING.

During our first session, I found these common patterns:

1. They referred to the customer segment as class A, B, C, or D.

2. They shared a lot about their solution, but when asked about the problem, they had very few words to describe it.

3. There was this unanimous unsupported consensus that targeting the A or B class is much easier than any other segment.

4. The same unanimous unsupported consensus was that targeting corporate customers (B2B) was much more convenient/profitable than retail customers (B2C).

5. They had minimum interaction with their customers.

That is an interesting observation because it displays the fact that founders don't put enough emphasis on understanding the customers' points of view and build products that no one really needs. I've always asked the entrepreneurs to share more details about their co-founders and founding team in the Google form. The results were often varied and very interesting. The key takeaway here is that many entrepreneurs often spend exorbitant amounts of time on products that they "think" will fill a need just because they have a good idea. However, without validation, that is hard to prove.

Key Insight 5

~40%

OF THE ENTREPRENEURS SEEKING MY MENTORING SESSIONS WERE SOLO FOUNDERS.

These were the common threads that tied them together:

1. Most of them were male with a background related to a family business.

2. Most of the male founders were looking to find the "perfect" co-founder but were not able to.

3. The female founders preferred to lead alone, citing unpleasant experiences with previous co-founders.

4. Only one female founder was a coder. The remaining founders were focused on the business side of things; especially marketing and business development.

The key takeaway here is that male founders preferred to have support in the form of a co-founder while female founders preferred to have independence in the form of working alone.

Key Insight 6

~27%

FEMALE FOUNDERS REPRESENTED AROUND 27% AND WERE SEEKING TO GROW THE BUSINESS.

These are the common observations among them:

1. A common observation about female founders is that they performed much better than male founders in discipline and dedication to the startup.

2. Female founders showed more interest in learning in general with a specific focus on validation.

3. Female founders also seemed less focused on getting funded and more interested in making sales and growing their businesses organically.

From this, we can see that there is a certain level of drive and determination present in female founders that is not necessarily organically there in male founders. While this can and usually is cultivated throughout the learning process, female founders tend to have more of a sense of direction and independence.

Reflections On The Key Insights

Despite using the lean methodology vocabulary, I see little of the mindset implemented in discovering value. In other words, far too many entrepreneurs rush into their product launches without having done enough groundwork to ensure that they have actually learned enough about the value behind their products. While there is merit in the saying "jump and build your plane on the way down," there are far too many entrepreneurs who end up following a wasteful and expensive "waterfall" approach to fix their products post-launch.

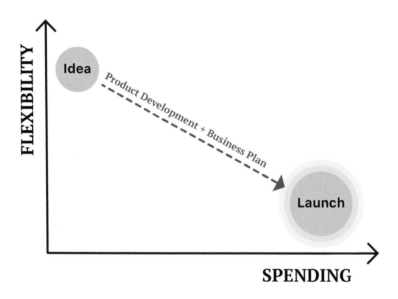

Figure 1: The Risky Investor Pleasing Journey

The common approach is to build a product and write a business plan or create a pitch deck to impress investors. This equation of product development plus business plan offers founders nothing but a high-risk approach to building a business. By rushing to build products and pitch decks, founders don't realize that they are quickly maximizing spending and minimizing flexibility to make changes. I like to call that the rushed decline towards launching a startup. This is the speedy decline in the ability to make changes coupled with the substantial decrease in cash availability.

When I realized that founders were using lean startup vocabulary and not the approach, I knew that the ideas behind them were not well understood. Instead, they were used to prove a point, win an argument, and glorify a behavior. There are definitely a lot of aspects missed, which led me to consider another common dimension of these results. I found that forcing a startup to happen by rushing the idea to launch with a working product and a business plan had a psychological component – in many cases dominating the business side of the uncertain journey of entrepreneurship.

This is precisely how I came to the postulation that the uncertain journey of entrepreneurship is comprised of two distinct journeys: the mindset and the startup journeys, as previously mentioned. These journeys are braided together in a way that can be easily mistaken for one journey.

As I progressed in my understanding of both journeys, connecting those repeating patterns that were commonly observed, I realized that each journey could have a distinct system of progress.

Hence, my theory was developed further. The uncertain journey of entrepreneurship is made of two distinct journeys with two distinguishable systems of progress. These systems of progress affect each other constantly and repeatedly. They are systems of learning that, with the right amount of attention, can help any founder make the fitting progress on their uncertain journey of entrepreneurship.

With a clear understanding of the concepts behind this book and an introduction to the tools that you are going to be exposed to, we can conclude this chapter.

Exercise 1:
Remember Why I Am Here

This simple exercise is a reminder of why you started your startup. Sometimes, all you need is to remember why you started it – something to reignite your passion for it.

Setting   Choose a quiet place.

Tools   Pen, paper, and your favorite beverage (and maybe cookies, too).

Type   Personal exercise.

When   During a setback to your startup. Once you finish it, hang it where you can see it often, like on your bathroom mirror. It is a helpful reminder.

Exercise Steps:

1 Write down five reasons why you started your startup.

2 Once you are done, take another five minutes to reflect on what you wrote down by asking yourself:

  - Am I still doing this for the same reasons I started it?
  - If not, then what changed?
  - If yes, then what was my motivation behind each of them?

3 Now, sit down, relax your mind, focus on these five reasons, and remember all the energy and passion when you had your start moment.

AT THIS POINT, I'M GOING TO MOVE ON AND TAKE YOU THROUGH THE FIRST OFFICIAL PART OF THE GUIDE: THE MINDSET JOURNEY.

1

The Mindset Journey

"

Work on the mindset, and creating a successful startup is only a matter of time!

Advice I offer to entrepreneurship
support program teams.

03
The Mindset Journey

When I began working with entrepreneurs, my main focus was on the business side of things. I mean, what else can a business mentor offer entrepreneurs? But then came those frequent, repetitive moments where I felt that something was impeding their progress. It wasn't the business; nor was it the surrounding or environmental challenges per se. This is when I had the sneaking suspicion that there was more to be found in paying attention to the human behind the entrepreneur than the business elements. As I began doing this, I sought clues as to what seemed to be an invisible component of the uncertain journey of building a startup.

At this point, I'm going to share my observations, insights, and stories from the field about the mindset journey of entrepreneurship. I will walk you through several events, patterns, and distinctive moments that arose from encounters with many of the entrepreneurs I mentored. It is my attempt to make sense of everything I witnessed.

I also respect the privacy of my entrepreneurs. Yes, all the stories you will read in this book describe real-life events. However, I won't necessarily share the exact information about those entrepreneurs themselves or their startups. My aim is to focus on the lessons behind the stories, not the identity of the people in them. As such, please be aware that I have made an effort to make the founders' personalities in my examples unrecognizable.

The Four Mindset States

As our first port of call on the mindset journey, I want you to think about something for a moment. What can you observe if you put a potato and an egg in boiling water? Well, the potato becomes mushy and you can easily remove its skin. The egg, on the other hand, hardens on the inside while it remains easily breakable on the outside.

What does that tell you?

Two different elements under the same conditions can have very different results.

Now, what happens if you keep them both in the boiling water for an extended period? They both become inedible, lose all their nutrients, and have useless shapes.

Becoming an entrepreneur is not about being hard like an egg or soft like a potato when exposed to challenging conditions. Instead, it is to learn when you need to be hard like an egg and when you need to soften like a potato. But that's not all. It is also about knowing when to get out of the boiling water and when to get back in. Moreover, this parable indicates that not all entrepreneurs are the same. They learn and perceive differently. They all go through the four mindset states during different phases of their journey. What's important to note is that the combination of those states creates the mindset journey and each mindset state has repeating attributes, thus, creating noticeable patterns.

When I was figuring out the mindset states that founders go through on their journey, I was in the pursuit of developing a simple framework that could clearly display how founders learn in the context of how they perceive the world around them. All of my notes pointed towards a direct relationship between the way that founders learn and the way they perceive the world around them while they are learning. One thing was for certain: they both undeniably impacted each other.

During my research, I came across the work of Don Kelley and Daryl Conner, who created what we know as the Emotional Cycle of Change [2]. This model describes the five steps of the emotional response of a person going through change. Essentially, Kelley and Conner describe the five-step cycle by highlighting how it can affect a person on an emotional level and drive behaviors. This model became the launchpad for the Four Mindset States framework.

As I said earlier, the framework displays the relationship between the founders' learning and how they perceived the world while learning.

Both sides have equal weight and they contribute relatively to the resultant mindset state of the founder in the context of the uncertain journey of entrepreneurship. Founders can perform much better if they work on their perception and how they learn. Both are skills that founders can, in time, learn to manage and harness for their own benefit and mindset progress.

With this understanding of the entrepreneur's mindset, let's begin exploring the four mindset states in broader detail.

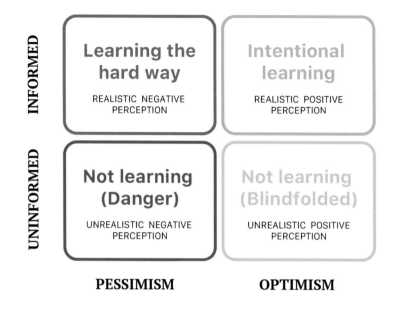

Figure 2: The Four Mindset States of The Entrepreneur

The Four Mindset States Are:

1 *Uninformed Optimism (UO):* When embracing this mindset state, founders are not in the process of learning with an unrealistic positive perception of the world. It is an innocent mindset embraced mainly at the start of the journey. It can also be attributed to the allure of the "new" and all of the potential it has to offer. Indeed, in this mindset state, founders are considered blindfolded.

2 *Informed Pessimism (IP):* When embracing this mindset state, founders are in the process of learning the hard way with a realistic perception of the world. It is the "suffering for the cause" part of the journey.

③ *Informed Optimism (IO):* When embracing this mindset state, founders are capable of Intentional Learning with a realistic view and a positive outlook of the world. It is the spirited and balanced part of the journey where entrepreneurs perform at their best.mindset state, founders are considered blindfolded.

④ *Uninformed Pessimism (UP):* When embracing this mindset state, founders are not learning with an unrealistic view and a negative world outlook. It is the "suffering for absolutely no reason" part of the journey. It is unnecessary and sometimes dangerous and should be avoided.

Each mindset state reflects the entrepreneurs' ability to learn, extract insights, and apply them to upgrade their own perception of the world. When there is no learning, there is no perception upgrade, hence, there is no or minimal growth for the entrepreneur and, as a consequence, the startup.

Throughout this section of the book, I will use these four mindset states to describe the most commonly encountered founder mindset journeys. I aim to highlight the common blind spots that can be avoided when founders are conscious of them.

Uninformed Optimism (UO)

Being optimistically uninformed is perhaps the main reason most entrepreneurs embark on their startup journey in the first place [3]. They get an idea and set it as a destination worth pursuing, unaware of possible hurdles. That euphoric state of mind is mainly embraced at the early beginnings of an entrepreneur's startup journey [4].

In this mindset state, entrepreneurs have an unrealistic positive perception of the world, tailored to fit their own wishes and desires [5]. This is coupled with a superficial understanding of some of the general concepts behind their idea and that often gives them a boost of overconfidence. They are usually referred to as the "plan" or, sometimes, the "strategy."

Within this mindset state, entrepreneurs tend to overanalyze events taking place on their journey. They tend to translate adverse circumstances into a "temporary unfortunate setback that I will overcome" or as "good fortune". You might find an entrepreneur adopting an "it was about time" line of thinking if it was a positive outcome. In both cases, the entrepreneurs are not learning [6]. They go through their journey completely blindfolded with a reactive, unrealistic perception of the world.

Uninformed Optimism is indeed a reactive state of mind. Its embrace of unrealistic positivity consumes an entrepreneur's energy and spirit. Most entrepreneurs confuse unrealistic positivity with staying positive despite the journey's hardships. The difference is that the first is reactive while the second is empowering. The first consumes energy and spirit like a black hole in space, while the second directs energy to the most practical area of usage.

As observed, this mindset state is usually a prelude to Uniformed Pessimism. Eventually, most founders move from not learning to learning the hard way while their perception slowly, but surely, goes from unrealistic positivity to realistic negativity.

Uninformed Optimism (UO) Manifestation

One of the most interesting manifestations of Uninformed Optimism is when an entrepreneur has a very nice logo for his startup before having a well-rounded concept of value (for/from the customer). Almost all entrepreneurs with assumed problem- solution fit startups, who requested a mentoring session, submitted a very nice logo on the session request Google form. However, they offered superficial input about the startup, the value proposition, and the customer.

Another interesting manifestation is the "I have an answer to any question" behavior. This case is overwhelmingly frequent among entrepreneurs with an Uninformed Optimism mindset state. Many of them focus on giving answers but not on asking questions. They offer arguments but with very little proof. Also, they usually have a good story that has been carefully developed over time and modified after interactions with judging panels and mingles with mentors. Of course, it will all be displayed with extreme confidence and a huge smile. I always try to showcase to these entrepreneurs that arguments are not really answers to questions. Good answers come from in-depth research and great ones come from data-supported validation activities in the field.

A final significant manifestation of Uninformed Optimism is represented in how some entrepreneurs seek to find personal validation by getting the approval of investors and mentors. Many entrepreneurs confuse the verification of the idea by a well-known mentor, investor, or entrepreneur with personal confirmation and something to be proud of.

They follow what I like to call the "startup death loop" with that kind of approach.

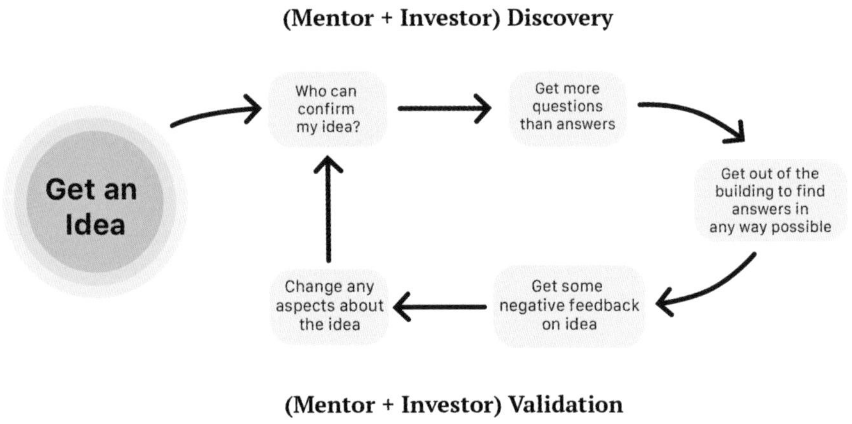

(Mentor + Investor) Discovery

Get an Idea

Who can confirm my idea?

Get more questions than answers

Get out of the building to find answers in any way possible

Change any aspects about the idea

Get some negative feedback on idea

(Mentor + Investor) Validation

Figure 3: Often Observed Phenomena in UO: The Startup Death Loop

In Steve Blank's Customer Development Approach [7], founders focus on validating their startup idea by interviewing customers and finding insights that can help them define the problem or challenge that a specific customer segment is facing. This phase is referred to as Customer Discovery. Once They have enough insights, founders propose a solution and engage in customer validation activities, in which they attempt to understand the customer's perspective on their proposed solution and their willingness to pay for it. This phase is referred to as Customer Validation.

Entrepreneurs with an Uninformed Optimism mindset state tend to seek idea confirmation from people they perceive as legitimate instead. They start researching and ask themselves "Who would be a good source of confirmation for my idea?" They go around displaying an unfinished and under-researched idea to reputable entrepreneurs, mentors, and investors. Instead of that coveted confirmation, they get comments, critiques, and sometimes cynical, rude responses. They keep at it until they reach a well-polished version of their presentation of the still unfinished, under-researched idea. They perform what I like to call Mentor/Investor Discovery (instead of Customer Discovery). They, therefore, validate their startup ideas without involving their customers.

Once they have a hyped-up pitch deck with a cool startup logo and a catchy slogan, they tend to go directly for investment. They feel confident that they are armed with all of the right answers to win an argument with the investors during the pitch Q&As. So, they approach investors rigorously with the still underdeveloped idea, and all the big names are highlighted as mentors at the end of the well-polished pitch deck. They usually get negative feedback from investment committees and competition panels. So, they go back to the mentors and ask them this often-used question: "Tell me what I need to say to investors to get funded?" They perform what I like to call Mentor/Investor Validation (instead of Customer Validation).

They keep changing aspects of the idea and the pitch deck – adding or removing features and religiously looking for idea confirmation. Eventually, most of them run out of money and steam to continue. I say most of them because some get lucky in finding initial funding. This is perhaps the most frequently observed and shortest startup journey that first-time, early-stage entrepreneurs can go through.

During my first mentoring session with founders seeking opinions to confirm ideas versus having questions to explore value, I always respond with: "My opinion is not important. What will your customer do in this case?" When they run out of opinion-based arguments and I finally get an "I don't know," I ask them to go and find out.

If you find that you're in this phase, you can avoid the startup death loop by seeking to explore and asking questions frequently. The more you focus on the answers as opposed to the questions, the more you kill the potential of your startup. Do you know why? Because without questions, you are limiting the potential of your imagination. The potential of your startup is only limited by your imagination.

Ask questions first and then be curious to find answers.

Informed Pessimism (IP)

Informed Pessimism is perhaps the most observed mindset among entrepreneurs who manage to keep their startup alive for nine months or more. It is the mindset where the perception has changed as they've realized that things are not really as positive as assumed. It is at this stage that they continue getting hit by the grinding nature of building a startup [8]. The heavy burdens of uncertainty combined with little or no safety net quickly become an alternate reality to the euphoria associated with a new idea and all the potential it represents.

In this frame of mind, entrepreneurs are in the process of learning the hard way. In other words, the perception is bombarded with the hard tests first, followed by the lessons [9]. In many observed cases, entrepreneurs don't get the lesson entirely from the first time around and take more than one trial to get a well-rounded understanding. After some time within such an environment, the entrepreneurs become gradually less positive and more inclined towards a negative interpretation of events.

Learning the hard way is a trial-by-fire learning process, where experiences accumulate rapidly but are not always fully digested. The dramatic increase in challenging situations combined with the negatively inclined outcomes forces most entrepreneurs to move from digesting insights in order to grow to more of a learning-to-survive attitude. Perhaps that is why most entrepreneurs begin to have more negative interpretations of the outcomes of events before they actually occur. It is more of an "I don't want to get disappointed" kind of thing than being negative. In other words, trial by fire pushes entrepreneurs to self-preserve against any potentially expected disappointment or loss.

But that is not all. This experience-based learning seems to be associated with an even faster accumulation of emotional scars or unforgettable negative associated feelings. As founders keep getting rejections, face demeaning interactions with stakeholders, and constantly get last-minute curveballs, all associated emotions with those events quickly become the frame of reference from which future decisions are made.

Mentoring Notes

Entrepreneurship is essential for the world to innovate and prosper. We, as a community, should embrace our entrepreneurs as human beings and not just as idols if they are successful and has-beens if they are not. The worst thing about a failed startup is that the scars that come with the journey don't stop with the cease of operations. They linger and can only be healed with time, support, and non-judgmental ears. Offer founders support, even if their startups shut down.

Informed Pessimism is perhaps one of the most challenging components of the mindset journey. It is where the entrepreneurs' faith in their ideas – as well as in each other as a team – is tested most aggressively. Choosing the right people to join a startup journey is as critical as the idea pursued. It is often observed that many entrepreneurs overlook this issue. They embark on journeys with non-compatible co-founders just for the sake of starting. Think long and hard before you let someone join your journey.

In some cases, Informed Pessimism can be the prelude to Informed Optimism. However, it is often interrupted by the abrupt end of the startup journey and the shutting down of the business. Founders who continue and, eventually, get to the Informed Optimism stage are those who were able to pass that part of the startup journey, whether by a lucky circumstance that saved them or via their own last-minute epiphanies about how to push forward. In both cases, they were able to have enough time to start reflecting on their experiences and use what they have learned to ask better questions.

Informed Pessimism (IP) Manifestation

One big sign of Informed Pessimism is how entrepreneurs become fixated on what they have experienced and how it made them feel. Harsh experiences become a primary frame of reference [10]. Founders become focused on what they know and dread reencountering it. That creates a direct relationship between how deeply they were scarred and how much they fear it.

However, when that point was reached, I observed a fascinating phenomenon. This group of entrepreneurs is divided into two types: those who learned fear and those who learned *despite* fear. The first type of entrepreneur will allow the fear of what they have learned to stop them from making real progress [11]. Fear has blinded their perception and forced them to interpret the events happening with unrealistic, relatively negative views. The impact on productivity and energy is significant. Decision-making is postponed and prolonged as much as possible, especially with any critical move.

The second type, however, has manifested what I like to call fear-fueled courage [12]. When entrepreneurs reach the point of overwhelming fear, they throw everything they have at it instead of standing still. They keep doing it until they are no longer afraid. Fear has motivated their perception to discover a way out. In essence, fear has acted as a catalyst for learning instead of performing a mindset death grip. Hence, the perception is encouraged to look at previously confronted challenges with less of an experience-based interpretation. It replaces them with more pragmatic and progress-focused views.

The first type can be guided to push through and become like the second with some support and active listening. Well, at least some of the first type; not all.

Consider jumping in a pool from a high diving board for the first time. The experience can be daunting. If it was not pleasant, that might cause the jumper to be reluctant to do it again. Now, suppose that the second and third trials offer similar bad experiences. In that case, the jumpers' perception will be calibrated to that negative experience. They will not feel the urge to jump again unless they absolutely have to. Now, let us assume that they meet with an experienced jumper that we will call EJ. After spending some time listening to the experience from the perspective of the jumpers, EJ understands that the experience wasn't totally bad; only some components of it were. Those negative components, however, have overshadowed the whole thing. So, EJ shares some tips about the angle and speed of the jump that can reduce the impact that the jumpers make on the surface of the water. Finally, the jumpers realize that they can do something about it. At this moment, the darkness of fear is illuminated with new and untried approaches.

In some cases, Type 2 entrepreneurs can reach a point of exhaustion in facing fear with courage. This burnout can be expected and should not be confused with quitting or surrendering. They must be encouraged to take some personal time to recharge and reflect, even if it means that work will suffer from delays.

Another practical manifestation in the field is what I like to call Bridge-less Island Behavior. Despite being one of the least obvious ones, I have been observing it with increasing frequency in the past few years. In this case, the entrepreneurs isolate themselves from the world. They prefer the companionship of Netflix to that of other people. They do the minimum amount of work possible throughout their day and rush back to their homes where they spend time with Friends – the hit show; not the real ones. If they can perform all of their duties remotely, they will absolutely opt for this option.

This self-enforced isolation is usually caused by the rising sense of overwhelming vulnerability in an unsafe environment. Entrepreneurs, especially solo founders, stay away from friends and family because they don't want the guilty feelings associated with worrying them. Plus, they definitely don't want to get the "I told you so" lecture. In both cases, those entrepreneurs feel isolated in their feelings and thoughts. They can't share them. As a mentor, when I notice these patterns happening, I do my best to communicate that I am available. I also try to share some stories about other entrepreneurs, without mentioning names, who have also gone through similar situations. I do my level best to point out that they are not alone and that others go through the same phase. It makes them feel more normal and less guilty about feeling like they are letting themselves down as well as their teams, their families, and perhaps, their investors – to all of whom the entrepreneurs can't express what they think and feel.

I also give them exercises where they will have to express themselves by either painting, free-writing, playing music, or just free dancing. If they can't express themselves in words to others, they should let it out in some other way. I rarely mention working out because it feels like homework and is often not an enjoyable or fun activity to try.

Mentoring Notes

If you ever encounter an entrepreneur going through isolation, don't let them succeed at it! By just being there, they will respond. It is not about you but more about them. So, pay attention, listen, and understand. The idea is not to let them feel afraid to show their vulnerability to you as a mentor. By all means, don't try to get them off their island of isolation. Instead, extend a bridge of active listening and nonjudgmental friendship. If the matter persists, professional help must be introduced as soon as possible.

Another manifestation of Informed Pessimism is what I like to call Startup Guilt. Many entrepreneurs feel guilty because of their startups. For example, many prefer not to spend money on anything personal because the "startup might need it." Some entrepreneurs forgo medical treatment because it is expensive. They have the money, but they stress about the fact that "the startup comes first."

Another manifestation of "startup guilt" is when entrepreneurs reach a point where they feel guilty about having a weekly day off. They don't want to miss anything happening at the startup. They become obsessed and start hoarding higher workloads. They keep at it until they eventually burn out.

An extreme example that I only encountered once during my decade of mentoring entrepreneurs is the guilt of sleeping! One entrepreneur felt guilty that she was wasting her time sleeping despite only sleeping for four hours a day on average. Needless to say, she eventually crashed and almost needed to be hospitalized.

When entrepreneurs get fixated, they don't learn. When they get obsessed, they let go of flexibility. And when they stop acknowledging mistakes, they don't grow. Finally, negativity takes over the perception when all elements (lack of learning flexibility and growth) are combined.

Informed Optimism (IO)

Informed Optimism happens when entrepreneurs can move from learning the hard way to intentional learning. In learning the hard way, the test comes before the lesson. It is like sitting for your final exams at school without knowing that you have an exam. You complete the exam and, once you get your graded sheet back, you learn where your shortcomings were and then consider how you can improve.

Intentional Learning takes a completely different approach. Entrepreneurs are prepared by constantly asking what they need to learn to move forward. Intentional Learning is about asking questions whose answers can develop one's perception. They are questions that are more inclusive of surrounding perceptions. It is a condition where you are more respectful of your perception's limitations and in which you are diligent in seeking thoughts and opinions that are different from your own. Intentional Learning is equivalent to the freedom of the mind. In other words, you get to free your mind of what is convenient and familiar. You have the freedom to explore and appreciate what is new and uncommon. Simply put, you're in a position to ask questions to learn.

When this becomes a habit, it will allow you to get a glimpse of the approaching lessons before their tests. Asking questions will buy you time to better prepare for coming challenges. You will be less reactive and more preemptive on your journey.

But asking questions alone is not enough, even with embracing different perspectives together. You need to unlearn all the emotional side effects of previous tough lessons, with particular emphasis on those lessons that were learned in the hardest of ways. It is critical to free the perceptions from the heavy burden of negative emotions associated with experience-based lessons.

Informed Optimism is reached when entrepreneurs realize that learning is their true superpower and that it all starts from training the perception. Everything that happens on their journey is an input that can continuously upgrade their perception. It is okay to have associated feelings, whether negative or positive. For example, it is only natural and human not to feel good when rejected by investors. Entrepreneurs in the Informed Optimism stage see rejection from investors as "we don't have the answers yet to convince them." So, they ask for advice and insist on feedback to do better on their next attempt. Understand that the feelings associated with rejection are momentary if you decide to make them so. Don't set those feelings in stone and, more importantly, don't make them the correlated defaults when that situation repeats itself.

Ultimately, Informed Optimism offers entrepreneurs the knowledge that perception can empower or enslave them. It all depends on how the learnings, which were accumulated throughout the journey, are perceived. When learning becomes the limit of what you know, your perception will become a limiting boundary to your mindset's progress. In other words, when you become only sure of what you think you know, you become unable to open up to new learnings. This is especially true if it comes in the form of a critique delivered in a time of pressure. So, focusing only on what you think you know will not help you build a realistic view of the world!

When you realize that what you know is simply a confirmation of how much you don't know, your attitude and behavior change entirely. You become more open to view the perceptions of others and learn. You become more attentive to the world and can see it as a galaxy of perceptions; not the black hole of your opinions. The less you acknowledge the importance of people's perception of the world in creating the reality around you, the more limited and unrealistic your view of the world becomes.

When this recognition of limitation is combined with fast and attentive learning habits, it empowers you with a liberating sense of freedom. Not being sure of everything has the power to make us realize that we can't control everything. Control is indeed an illusion in the context of building a startup. Realizing that will allow you to focus not on what you can do but on how you can respond and, most importantly, how you can always become prepared by continuously extracting insights from your learnings and using them to modify your perception constantly.

Not knowing everything liberates our minds from the logic- shadowing effects of assumptions. We assert our faith in our ability to harness insights and apply them to make progress. We become truly open to learning and ready to progress on the journey at that moment. That is how the Informed Optimism mindset is reached.

Informed Optimism (IO) Manifestation

Perhaps one of the most common manifestations of the Informed Optimism mindset is that calm urge to reflect and think when something new or unexpected happens. In this instance, I would get a phone call and the caller would request a session to think and reflect on a specific situation. He is not looking for advice, not asking for feedback, and definitely not looking for support. He seeks to upgrade his perception of the situation by viewing it through another. This is an interesting ping-pong session where one neutral view of the world helps another see the world in HD quality.

Another manifestation of Informed Optimism is when entrepreneurs stop relying on just intuitions. Intuition can serve as a starting point when making decisions, but most definitely not as an end. They appreciate it as a hypothesis but not as fact. They highlight it as a hypothesis and seek to support it with tangible proof. To move from relying on intuition in decision-making to using it as the starting point to discover and progress is one of the best manifestations of Informed Optimism.

Mentoring Notes

Founders in the Informed Optimism (IO) stage require more listening than talking. They are not looking for answers from their mentors. Instead, they seek someone to help them see and appreciate different perceptions, especially when they can't. They will ask a lot of questions, but it is a mentor's job to help them ask better, more meaningful questions and to be there while they attempt to find answers.

Uninformed Pessimism (UP)

Perhaps this is the most critical mindset state that any entrepreneur can be in. It is the mindset embraced when the perception tends to interpret everything negatively. Because they are not learning, entrepreneurs are repeatedly faced with a severe collision between perceived reality and – well – reality! That paints negative influences on the mindset because nothing explains why.

As entrepreneurs focus on making things work instead of learning why they are not working, they continue to suffer from the constant collisions between their perception of reality and actual reality. This will continue to happen with a growing impact on the entrepreneur's mental well-being.

If you feel like you are going through this phase, you should consider seeking professional help. Asking for help and support is a display of love and appreciation for yourself. Demonstrate self-love and appreciation by seeking out support from friends, family, and people around you who care for and appreciate you.

Uninformed Pessimism (UP) Manifestation

A general sign of uninformed pessimism is when entrepreneurs emphasize emotions over thoughts and prioritize how they feel over anything else. When you interact with entrepreneurs who are in the midst of Uninformed Pessimism, you will find that their feelings are strong and sometimes expressed with excess. The negative emotions appear in a masked format at first. Still, they quickly take shape into a more apparent and expressive form.

For example, one of the cases I encountered was a charming person transforming into a sarcastic personality. It was displayed, at first, in the form of jokes. The jokes quickly became criticism and, finally, this transformed into lashing-out sessions. The darker it gets, the harder it becomes for entrepreneurs to hide it. But it also becomes more challenging for them to ask for help or see anything in a positive context.

Mentoring Notes

In Informed Pessimism, entrepreneurs learn the hard way. They live the consequences of all the hard lessons they had to go through. Most importantly, they know why they are going through a tough time. They can ask for help because they know when the load is too heavy to carry alone. But in the case of Uninformed Pessimism, the entrepreneur's perception is entirely hijacked by the way it feels and not the why. Feelings become the only input the perception feeds on. So, reasoning with them is not a good strategy. Offering to help is not a good idea either. You must make yourself available and wait until they are ready to ask. In that case, I offer them a list of different mental health professionals to do some research and schedule a session with. I also offer to come along for their first appointment and stay in the waiting area to make them feel safer. Mentors should give time and focus when they meet someone manifesting symptoms of Uninformed Pessimism. However, they should offer the time and attention in a supporting capacity next to professional help.

Reflections on The Mindset States

Entrepreneurship is not for everyone. Yes, not everyone can meet the demands of the journey and how it can impact them. However, entrepreneurship should be human too. We should not forget about those who suffer to accomplish as we celebrate the winners. We must offer them the right support system, including the best mental support we can afford. We should value the conquerors but also care for the wounded as a community. How we treat those who aren't praised or influential says a lot about us.

Uninformed and Informed Pessimism Mindset States are both very painful for anyone to go through alone. In some extreme cases, entrepreneurs clearly mentioned their desire to end their lives. These were some of the saddest moments in my journey as a mentor.

The truth is that many entrepreneurs go through it all alone, especially the new and inexperienced ones. The mental effects should be highlighted when explaining entrepreneurship to first-timers, and clear support options should be offered.

Ultimately, the mindset journey begins subconsciously but with the conscious decision to initiate a startup journey. The first step on the progress meter is, therefore, to realize that you are actually taking the very first steps on your mindset journey. Being oblivious will always put you in a position where your mindset is reacting to external events and situations. You will always be surprised and underprepared.

By reading these words, I would like to congratulate you on realizing that you are actually on your mindset journey. The first step is done!

The second step is to realize that your perception of the world needs to be constantly upgraded but, more importantly, you must learn to be patient. As you progress on the startup journey, you will start to encounter many challenging events and unexplained rejections and, in many cases, it can also be a demeaning experience. Please understand that it is just a matter of teaching your perception patience. Sometimes, the world doesn't reveal everything you need to know all at once; it takes its time. When your perception is rushed, it can generate unnecessary thoughts, thus, burdening your mindset with uneasy emotions and feelings. By allowing yourself time to fully perceive a particular situation around you from different perspectives and with fewer self-judgments, you will better understand the world.

	Uninformed Optimism	Informed Pessimism	Informed Optimism	Uninformed Pessimism
Definition	Not learning with an unrealistic positive perception of the world.	Learning with a realistic but negative perception of the world.	Intentional learning with a realistic and positive perception of the world.	Not learning with an unrealistic but negative perception of the world.
Founder State	Blindfolded founders.	Learning the hard way founders.	Intentional learning founders.	Founders in danger.
Manifestations	A very nice logo for his startup before having a well-rounded concept of value (for/from the customer).	Become fixated on what they have experienced and how it made them feel.	Founders act with a calm urge to reflect and think when something new or unexpected happens.	Founders emphasize emotions over thoughts and prioritise how they feel over anything else.
	"I have an answer to any question" attitude. Founders focus on giving answers but not on asking questions. Offering a lot of arguments but very little proof.	Two types of founders emerge: Those who learned fear and those who learned despite fear.	Founders stop relying on just intuitions. They appreciate it as a hypothesis but not as fact. They highight it as a hypothesis and seek to support it with tangible proof.	Founders express strong vfeelings and with excess.
	Founders find personal validation by getting the approval of well-known investors and mentors.	Bridge-less Island behavior. Founders isolate themselves from the world.	Founders are seeking to ask better questions with the help of mentors.	Transformation into a sarcastic lashing-out personality.
		Startup Guilt. Founders suffering constant guilt.		Inability to hide the negative publicly.

Table 1: Summary of the Four Mindsets of Entrepreneurship

Practicing Perception Patience

In 2018, I was contacted by two co-founders who were already three years into their startup journey. They were good friends and worked together perfectly well. They also worked really hard on building a solid startup. The thing is, the entrepreneurship ecosystem around them was not seeing fantastic friendship, hard work, and, surprisingly, not even the amazing results they had accomplished with the minimal available resources they had. The ecosystem was mostly fixated on the founders' relatively humble background, the local university they graduated from, the untrendy way they dressed, and the heavy accent when they spoke in a foreign language. The founders always felt unwelcome in events, pitching competitions, and entrepreneurship programs. When I asked them why they needed my mentorship, they gave me a very long monologue that didn't have any clear answer on how I could best help them or what they were expecting to gain from my knowledge.

I dedicated time to listen to what they had to say. My aim was to help them explore the different possible reasons they felt they needed mentoring. One recurring observation during that period was that the founders were making a lot of effort to convince me that they were good enough. To tell you the truth, they were more than good enough. They were great – awesome even. They loved their work and cared about the people on their team. Their business was going steady and growing. Yet, for some reason, every time we talked about business, we went from discussing details of work to reflecting on specific events and situations. And they always displayed an uneasy feeling that something was wrong. Their perception was impacted by all the comments from their surrounding environment on how they dressed, spoke, and acted. All of that was translated into "we don't fit in" thoughts, thus, generating feelings of anguish, frustration, and – sometimes – anger. Their surrounding environment had become a constant burden and distraction. When I finally realized what was going on, I understood why they sought my mentorship in the first place. They were looking for a second opinion!

They wanted to find out whether the "not fitting in" stigma was merited or not and I can't blame them. It is unsavory for any respectable founder when all of their hard work and accomplishments are limited to how they dress and annunciate in a conversation.

It wasn't until the fall of 2021 that they realized they were actually incredible founders. They were raising funds for their Series A round. They were surprised that many international investors were interested in leading the round. Yes, you read that correctly: many international venture capital firms (VCs) were interested in leading their Series A fundraising round. They had been following the startup's progress and all of the great results. They saw the founders' potential as future leaders and wanted to invest in that.

In case you didn't get the moral of the story, let me share it with you. The founders' perception of themselves and their work was limited to how the world around them perceived them, and the world around them was giving higher priority to superficial aspects more than anything of substance when it came to evaluating them.

This is what the world around them prioritized in evaluating founders in general and not just them. If they had allowed their perception a little bit of patience, they would have reached the understanding that it was not about them as founders but rather about the surrounding environment. Their perception didn't get that result until they had the opportunity to contrast it with the perception of another evaluating environment. The local surroundings prioritized investments in what is perceived as the "right founders". In contrast, the international environment prioritized investments based on the founders with the right results. That distinction made all the difference for them.

So, the second step involves learning to develop your perception's patience with the least damage possible to your mindset journey. In other words, you should give yourself enough time and diverse input from the world around you before you make a final judgment of your perception of yourself.

While progressing on your startup journey, the mindset collects a lot of feelings and emotions that are nothing more than the results of perception-based thoughts. If the perception is limited, you must realize that the feelings induced by it are temporary and will change with the availability of more information. So, focus on perception-patience while you work hard on gathering more information and asking questions.

Don't limit your journey to the way it makes you feel. Nothing good can come out of that.

You want personal validation? Forget about all the contests you won with all the photos of big checks on social media. Forget about all of the mentors and advisors from international companies that you have in your court and forget about all the 25 Under 25 lists on which you made an appearance. These are nothing more than brief moments that are fast forgotten and quickly lose their significance.

Successful moments are the result of many unsuccessful attempts combined with patience and determination. Let that journey of patience and determination be the determining factor of your self-validation! Define yourself by how hard you were hit and how you decided to stand up and keep fighting – every time!

Self-validation should come from how you have creatively solved problems, empathetically and patiently empowered your team, diligently managed your startup in hard times and good times, and how you bootstrapped when you could have sprayed money around. These are all examples of self-validating moments that you should be proud of.

When you are in the top 25 Under 25 list or standing on the stage with this really large check or doing that first talk show about your startup's accomplishments, remember that all of it is nothing more than other people acknowledging your hard work. This means that you have clearly managed to push forward despite all of the challenges. But they are not self-validation moments; only public celebrations of your very private and often unseen self-validation moments.

Your personal validation must come from the moments when you realize that you have the upper hand on your perception. Your personal validation is the moment you defeat doubts in your mind, transform fear into motivation, and mentally blossom. This is your personal validation moment and nothing can take that away from you. Not even if your startup goes bankrupt or you feel like it has been defeated by the competition.

Nothing!

Reflections on Your Journey

Always remember that your mindset is your support system! During your journey as an entrepreneur, your mindset is your strongest asset to lean on for support and inspiration. Pay attention to its status (fresh/worked up/exhausted). Like your body, it requires monitoring, exercising, and constant development.

First things first, make sure you get enough sleep, eat healthy, and have time for personal reflection. Also, make sure that you have time for human interactions outside of work.

Secondly, self-inspire. Lift your spirit up and keep moving forward. Here are some of the suggestions I offer entrepreneurs during our mentoring sessions.

Rediscover your sources of inspiration.

It can be anything: sports, music, movies, books, or a conversation with someone special. It can be a walk on a beach, in a garden, or just out in open space. It can even be a night out with your friends.

When you find something that sticks, make a habit of it. Don't just do it once a month. Intentionally include sources of inspiration in your daily, weekly, and monthly routine. Then, surprise yourself! From time to time, surprise yourself with new experiences. Sample new kinds of food from different cultures, go sightseeing in a place that you have never seen before, and go for a run or walk in the early morning. You never know what you might discover, so embrace it with an open heart and mind.

Additionally, try old things in a new way. Do you sing? Make a video of it and post it online. Are you a good storyteller? Offer standup comedy shows to kids at a school. Do you like staring at the night sky? Use an app to identify the constellations and the different planets and learn about them. You don't have to be good at it to enjoy it. You can immerse yourself in anything that sparks joy within you without being an expert at it.

Practice a hobby. Again, it doesn't have to be something that you are good at but definitely something you enjoy. You can do this in a group or on your own, so, this could be painting, playing a musical instrument, modern dancing, or even group knitting. Whatever gives you a sense of freedom and personal expression. It also offers you something to look forward to other than your upcoming meetings with investors or customers.

This brings me to my next point: express yourself. Let it all out and do it regularly. The journey can be frustrating at times and most definitely humbling. So, at regular times of the week or month, make sure to write down everything that frustrates you. Consider it your journey's diary.

Penultimately, don't be a stereotype. Forget about the stereotype of the lone entrepreneur who works 24/7 on their startup. It is not the best approach to create something because of just how damaging and draining it can be to both your mindset and your startup. Being an entrepreneur does not mean that you are not alive anymore. Being an entrepreneur is being open to life, people, the world, and all the wonders that they have to offer. Marvel at the world and I promise you it will inspire you.

Finally, take care of your well-being and, when you can, help others to do the same. With this in mind, you can safely move on to the cycles of learning from both the mentor's and the founder's point of view.

"

The purpose
of learning isn't
to affirm our
beliefs;
it's to evolve our
beliefs.

Adam Grant

04
The Cycles
Of Learning

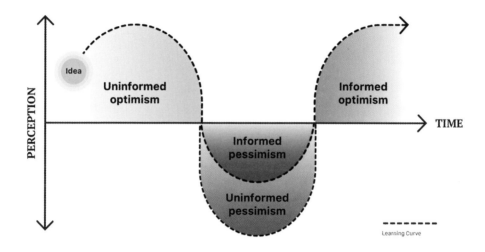

Figure 4: The Entrepreneur Cycles of Learning

The Four Mindset States described earlier don't come distinctively on their own. They come in series and, together, they create unique learning cycles for each entrepreneur. The time needed to move forward depends on the intensity of encountered experiences and the perception's ability to adapt and learn.

Now, I want to speak to mentors specifically on this. When it comes to mentoring entrepreneurs on the mindset journey, we must understand that this is the entrepreneurs' own personal journey. It has nothing to do with us. Our role as mentors is to help them navigate it with kind, sincere advice, and assured presence.

Because in the journey of entrepreneurship, there is a lot of judgment, both silent and apparent. Entrepreneurs will crave positive criticism that is delivered with kindness by someone they can trust. Entrepreneurs face judgment from their teams, investors, customers, support program employees, and other entrepreneurs. They also get a lot of praise when they are on the rise and a lot of indifference when they are not from those same groups of people. Having sincere conversations can center a human being like nothing else. Sincere words have the most amazing effects in helping entrepreneurs restore their inner balance, especially when they're feeling vulnerable.

From the Mentor's Point of View

A mentor becomes a safe haven – a place where there are no judgments; only active listening and a sincere exchange of knowledge and perceptions. In other words, mentoring sessions become an opportunity for entrepreneurs to express themselves. Sessions also provide a space in which entrepreneurs can feel that their perception is appreciated and be gently guided to see a situation from other perceptions.

The second component of the formula is the assured presence. To many entrepreneurs, knowing that they have access to their mentor is critical. They might not stay in touch, but when they call, a mentor must answer. In this kind of situation, a mentor is like a gas station: very critical to find when you are low on fuel, but not when the tank is full. As a mentor, make sure to be there for them before they run out of fuel. If you are not capable, then make sure to have a backup plan for them. It is essential to help entrepreneurs get a deeper understanding of the learnings of their journey and find insights in a relatable manner to their own cases. It is not a one-size-fits-all. It must be treated case by case.

If you can ensure that you're available to the entrepreneur, it will placate some of the anxieties that their environment may be putting them under. Now, I want to talk to the entrepreneurs again.

From the Founder's Point Of View

As an entrepreneur, you should know that there are no shortcuts on the mindset journey. It is more about absorbing the useful components of the experience in your own relative time and learning how to offload the intangible but harmful components in your own way. The mindset journey will come with many relatively dark emotions and stressful periods. It is then imperative to learn how to move forward without the heavy weight of these emotions. Basically, you'll need to embrace learning from experiences and unlearning the side effects.

You must take your time. It is not a destination you are racing to. Remember, it is more of a journey of incremental changes that happen really slowly. Moreover, these changes hide in the shadows of the swift and complicated ups and downs of the startup journey. That said, it is not about being flexible and going with the flow. However, it is equally not about being stiff in the face of complicated events. The journey is about your personal perception of the world and how it can become as practical as possible without compromising your positivity. It is a critical balance that is often hard to maintain and requires a lot of care.

As entrepreneurs, you must embrace the flow of the journey and make extracting insights from collected learnings your top priority. It should be closely followed by how it impacts your perception in a positive or negative manner as well as in a realistic or unrealistic manner.

Everything on the mindset journey happens in incremental doses. It is like when you decide to eat healthy and lose weight. You take a selfie of yourself every day to keep track of changes. If you compare the photo of day one with day two or even day ten, you won't notice much in spite of the fact that you were steadily losing around 400 grams every day. When will you start to see a difference? When you compare the day one photo with a photo six months later. Then, the change will be visible to the naked eye. The same thing happens to your mindset. It takes a long time to sense changes and it has to be seen from an outsider's perception – just as you do with the selfie of you.

Perhaps that is the primary role of having a mentor in the mindset journey: to help you see a snapshot of yourself periodically and offer guidance on how to manage incremental changes.

In 2018, I started working with an entrepreneur who was about to migrate from Uninformed Optimism to Informed Pessimism. Early signs of "learning the hard way" exhaustion began to overshadow the sunshine and dreamy feelings of starting something new. During our first few mentoring sessions, I noticed that transition emerging from her stories. She repeatedly delayed critical work. She sensed that all hard work would not be fruitful. She was getting a lot of rejections. When I shared my observation, she was really defensive. It was apparent that she was displeased. As the conversation continued, I gently explained the difference between Uninformed Optimism and Informed Pessimism mindset states. I also highlighted how normal it is for anyone building a startup to undergo these mindset state transitions – even experienced entrepreneurs.

It is a component of the journey that everyone has to go through, albeit with different variations. I stressed the "everyone" part of the conversation by giving many examples of other entrepreneurs, anonymously. As she began to feel calmer, I asked her to describe how her startup journey made her feel so far using only three words. I clearly remember that she gave me three synonyms for "fear". She was afraid to go forward with her idea and start implementing it in the real world. When we dug deeper, it wasn't because she had a negative perception of herself. It was simply because she was fixated on everything she didn't have – things that she thought were critical to her startup journey.

I asked her to make a table with only two columns. Then, I asked her to write "what I don't have" in the first column and "what I have" in the second one. When she had done this, I gave her five minutes to fill both columns with as many points as possible. She was to do this without overthinking or rationalizing.

"Just fill the columns," I said.

It took a couple of trials before she actually did it without letting her mind intervene. She had more things to help her start implementing her business than those that she didn't have, which was more than she thought she did. She asked me if I thought she could make it happen for real with eyes wide open. My usual reply in these cases is, "Ask your customers. My opinion is not that important". And she did. At her own pace, she slowly launched her brand all by herself and she did it without any funding and with a small team of two interns. She began her dream business and did a great job moving forward. She learned to move forward by doing her best with what she had. She also switched her mindset from seeking approval to seeking eye-opening answers in the field and by herself. She moved forward by asking better questions.

I am very proud of her. Despite the fact that she didn't score millions of dollars in funding from a famous venture capital (VC) fund, she made a great accomplishment on the mindset battlefront. That deserves an even bigger celebration.

She is conquering herself.

The Ideal Cycle of Learning

The cycles of learning happen when you combine different mindset states together. They will act as doorways to each other or preparation platforms for one another. For example, Uninformed Optimism usually serves as a prelude to Informed Pessimism. In some cases, it can be a stepping stone to Uninformed Pessimism. It really depends on the surrounding conditions and the entrepreneur's ability to learn and apply those learnings.

Another example is Informed Pessimism and it can offer the correct settings for Informed Optimism. It provides all that entrepreneurs need to move from learning the hard way to intentional learning. But it all depends on how an entrepreneur embraces the experience and what kind of support is available.

It should not be your target to seek Informed Optimism in the sense of a destination and, in so doing, try to avoid other types of mindset states. That is not the right way to look at it and it is not how it works either. To progress on the mindset journey, seek to see the contrast between the different mindset states and learn about yourself through the lens of each one of them. It is a process that will require your patience and acceptance, but it will reward you with a continuous upgrade of your perception. Eventually, this will allow you to develop a more empowered, realistic perception of the world that is translated into positive thoughts and actions.

Learning cycles will always continue to happen every time you begin a new journey of exploration. However, with experience, time, and a better understanding of yourself, you can minimize the intensity of each mindset state. You can also increase the number of extracted insights per learning experience in less time and apply them more efficiently.

The ideal cycle of learning occurs when the mindset transitions from Uninformed to Informed Optimism by going through Informed Pessimism. It is not a standard cycle and I rarely observe it in the real world. I only use it to represent the ideal transition and to serve as a benchmark – a template of the journey, so to speak.

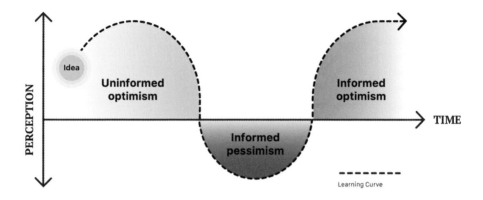

Figure 5: The Ideal Cycle of Learning

During my journey as a mentor, I have encountered several different cycles of learning with different mindset state combinations. I found that these combinations are greatly affected by the entrepreneur's perception state when they initiate the journey with that one decision to go ahead and build the startup.

Regardless, perception is the starting point for all cycles of learning. To start well, entrepreneurs must examine their perception when deciding to proceed with the startup journey. In the upcoming section of the book, I will shed more light on this. I will speak about the invisible power of perception, the different combinations of cycles of learning, and how the mindset journey evolves.

As we move further into more practical applications and peruse the tools that you will need to effectively navigate your startup journey, it's important to note that your mindset will continue to play a role in how this all unfolds. At this juncture, you will progress from the cycles of learning to the invisible power of perception.

"

Show me your questions. You show me your perception.

A statement I often start my mentoring session with.

05
The Invisible Power Of Perception

I would like to start this chapter with an example I heard from one of the founders I worked with. There was a man who owned a soap factory. He manufactured premium soap bars and packaged them into wonderfully designed soapboxes. Because of the excellent quality, the soap was in high demand. The man decided to ramp up the production to keep up with the increasing orders. Because the production line was operating at maximum capacity, sometimes the soap bars didn't end up in the packaging, and the boxes got shipped empty. Customers complained. So, the man got himself a consultant from a renowned consultancy firm to advise him on what to do. After a few days of investigative work, the consultant came back with a solution. He proposed the use of laser-based technology to monitor the weight of the soapboxes on the conveyor belt just before they went out to be shipped. That technology would cost the owner of the factory around $100,000.

"But it is a good investment," said the consultant.

The factory owner thanked him and saw him out before he went back to his office. Moments later, one of his factory floor workers knocked on his door and asked if he could have a moment of his time. But the factory owner was really bummed about the large sum of money he was about to spend and he was in no mood to chat. Nevertheless, he always prided himself on his open-door policy. So, he asked his employee in.

"I think I can save you a lot of money," the worker said.

The owner looked at him and asked what he was talking about. The employee seemed slightly embarrassed as he apologized for mistakenly overhearing the conversation his boss was having with the consultant. I have a better solution for you, and it will only cost you $100. Tomorrow, I will show you if you give me the money now and permit me to leave earlier today to prepare.

The owner smiled and decided to entertain the fantasy of his employee. He gave him the $100 and allowed him to leave early. The following day, the owner arrived at the factory, only to find his employee standing at the conveyor belt with a big smile on his face and a large fan. The owner asked him to show him his $100 solution. The employee asked a colleague to start the machine. As the soapboxes began to appear at the beginning of the conveying belt, the employee put the fan at maximum speed and made sure it was directed at the conveyor belt. The boxes with soap were unaffected and continued their journey to the other end of the belt peacefully. But the empty boxes simply flew off the belt and fell to the ground.

The employee looked at his boss with a big smile and said, "We only needed a $100 fan to solve our problem. "

This employee's perception translated the situation differently than the consultant's. In other words, He was able to view the issue at hand from a completely different angle than what is familiar and known. His simpler perception allowed him to explore the problem differently and uniquely. He didn't jump to what he knew or thoughts of what he didn't have. Instead, he looked at what it was that stood in front of him and how it could become better. He managed to find a more cost-efficient and easier solution for the problem at hand.

Perception is this invisible lens that, unknowingly, is installed over our eyes. It filters what we see according to a specific set of definitions. The more life experiences we encounter, the faster we define the world. Those definitions become the benchmarks – the filters – that make us focus on specific aspects of a particular situation and keep us utterly blind to others. They can also quickly become a confinement around our perception – a subconscious limitation to how we interpret and think of the world.

The uneasy fact here is that all of this happens subconsciously and without knowing that it is taking place. No one consciously works on how to perceive the world. It is something akin to muscle memory. It just happens with repetition. The more a particular type of event takes place, the more it will dominate the perception and become normal. It is like the first time you eat chocolate. You are wowed by the taste and may be surprised by the sweet lingering aftertaste. It becomes a sort of reward after a long day; maybe as a treat with your afternoon coffee. Soon enough, it becomes normal to have chocolate every day.

With entrepreneurs, perceptions work almost the same way but are more accelerated. Because of the fast-paced nature of the journey, founders gain experiences faster. In a relatively compressed time frame, perception can quickly be confined to a positive or negative interpretation of the world. It can soon be contained within a quick definition of the typical, familiar, and expected.

This reminds me of the spring of 2017.

Back then, I met with two founders working on a new Internet of Things (IoT) hardware startup during a session I was giving at a local university. They were both very enthusiastic young engineers and I could quickly tell that they were absolutely in love with their hardware. During our first mentoring session, the fresh graduates offered me a 15-minute monologue about all the excellent capabilities the hardware had and could possibly do. However, they said almost nothing about the customer or the market. As our sessions continued, I noticed that they had begun to consider other dimensions of their founders' efforts. Slowly but surely, they moved from fresh graduate engineers with a hardware project to entrepreneurs with a value proposition that contributed to solving a specific problem for a willing-to-pay customer segment.

So, those young, eager minds decided to seek initial funding. Armed with a working proof of concept and what promised to be a profitable and validated business model, they went around town to meet with possible investors. At that point, they had invested what little money they had in building the proof of concept and doing the validation activities. They absolutely needed the funding to move forward.

They had meetings scheduled with many famed angel investors and they got rejected from the first few. Nevertheless, they diligently accepted feedback and used it to develop and enhance their pitch. The rejections continued to pile up. Most of the time, without any explanations. But that was OK for them. They knew what they had signed up for and were going full speed ahead. As they continued to receive rejections, in some cases in regrettable ways, they slowly started to interpret the funding process negatively. I began to observe a change in the tone of our messages before they pitched new investors. Throughout one and half years, It slowly went from *"we will do our best"* to *"we will do our best, but we are not confident"* to *"we will do our best, but we know we will be rejected anyway."*

The unfortunate pitch with a well-known angel investor gave them the ultimate rejection of all rejections in history. The investor pounded them with scathing criticism – mainly directed at their person. They felt humiliated. It wasn't that their work was rejected, but they had confirmation that they were "not enough". And it came from a reliable source: a FAMED investor. It is regrettable, but it happened.

Now, here is the thing. It wasn't about any of that which they toiled to refine. It wasn't about the business model, nor the proof of concept, and most definitely not about their personal capabilities.

The fact is that, at the time they were making the pitch round, no one was eager to invest in a hardware company. It was something new to the local investors. They didn't have the right investment experience to evaluate the idea's potential. No local successful hardware startups could be used as a guiding example. All of these reasons rendered the investment to be hazardous in their eyes.

By the end of 2019, both entrepreneurs couldn't continue the journey and I couldn't blame them. In my humble opinion, these two extraordinary young minds did the work and created something wonderful. But it wasn't the right time – investment- wise. The downside of this story is that they left the journey thinking that they weren't good enough.

Within two years, they started from Uninformed Optimism and quickly moved to Informed Pessimism. Today, they are working on a new hardware startup. This time, they communicated their new product so that nontechnical investors could appreciate and evaluate it. They are also working smarter this time around; they are not limiting themselves to local investors. They are seeking out international investors who will guide them with hardware expertise and enough funding. They are doing a fantastic job.
So, in a nutshell, actions are the materialization of thoughts built on our perception's foundation. Thoughts can be accompanied by emotions, which can be a powerful determinant of potential actions. Sometimes, feelings are so strong, they actually prevail over the perception and confuse thoughts. It produces all the wrong actions.

It is always a matter of perception!

How you perceive your startup and the world, as well as how you perceive yourself, impacts your thoughts. Your thoughts will create your world, how you define it, and how you feel about it. They will generate expectations and materialize the boundaries of your ambitions and capabilities in your head. Once your thoughts come to an area where you have reached a decision, a

Figure 6: The Perception-Thought-Action Relationship

conclusion, or a plan, you move to the third and clear phase: you take action. Every time you progress on your mindset journey, **you take it one "perception to thought to action" at a time.**

Perceptions invoke thoughts.

Thoughts materialize into actions.

And a series of the right actions at the right time creates progress.

The starting point for my work as a mentor with entrepreneurs was perception. I realized that perception is the key to opening the unlimited potential of the mindset of entrepreneurs. That potential can have an incredible impact on the startup journey.

Every time entrepreneurs shared a filled business model canvas, they shared a visual representation of how they perceived the customer, the business, and how they both interacted.

And from that, I learned a lot about their perception!

Perception Presets

Over many years and hundreds of sessions with many different early-stage entrepreneurs, I realized that the starting perception of any entrepreneur had well-defined presets. In a way, the presets predefined how the entrepreneurs would go forward with their mindset journey.

Three types of presets are common and constantly observed in the field

1. Based on what entrepreneurs know, they go forward and implement their ideas.

2. Based on what entrepreneurs think they know, they seek what they think they **should know.**

3. Based on what entrepreneurs think they know, they seek what they think they **don't know.**

I aim to describe and point out the blind spots of founders who embrace those commonly observed "mindset presets." When blind spots are presented and explained, founders can work on altering and enhancing their perception and hence be able to make real progress on the mindset journey.

Perception Preset Type 1

BASED ON WHAT ENTREPRENEURS KNOW, THEY GO FORWARD AND IMPLEMENT THEIR IDEAS.

Perception Preset Type 1 is prevalent among engineers, inventors, and programmers. Because they are sure of what they know, their perception is blind to the potential of any exploration. Empowered with their knowledge, they go forward with plenty of power and certainty. They are embracing an Uninformed Optimism mindset state. Relatively speaking to the other types, founders embrace this mindset state the longest because they meet their potential customers relatively late. In the famous words of Steve Blank, the godfather of evidence-based entrepreneurship, the startup is inspired "inside the building". They seek investment early. So, they spend most of their time convincing investors with proof of concepts and projections spreadsheets rather than using customer validation from the field.

Engineers, inventors, and programmers turned entrepreneurs focus on implementation, not learning. When I discuss this topic with some of them, they always insist that they are learning plenty and they are learning for sure. However, they are learning about implementing a project rather than transforming an unvalidated idea into a business.

Any idea needs validation or a lot of research. For example, let us say you want to build a last-mile delivery app. There is little new data to explore regarding this kind of app. Everything you need to know as a founder has been discovered by existing startups in the market. Still, you will need to evaluate the market opportunity based on all you can learn from your research. To do that, you will need to understand the customers, the competition,In this mindset state, entrepreneurs have an unrealistic positive perception of the supply chain, and, of course, the potential profitability and investment needs. Then you can build the app!

For some reason, this is not what usually happens. Engineers, inventors, and programmers turning entrepreneurs expect investors to be happy with their assurance that they will succeed against the competition because they are capable of offering the same value for less money. Investors usually respond with the famous "show us proof of product-market fit (or customer stickiness), and then we talk investment." This polite brush-off is usually a sign of lousy research and validation work from Type 1 founders.

Under the influence of Uninformed Optimism, the founders go ahead, full steam ahead, with building the app. They borrow money from friends and family and spend it on initiating sales and online marketing activities. *They believe if they make the numbers, the investors will give them the needed funds.* And so, the quest for the holy grail begins!

When they finally engage the customer in the field, they realize how much they don't know. The first thing they recognize is that the app itself was – relatively speaking – the easy part. There is so much they have to do offline to make the online service function properly. On top of that, the customer has directly compared them with other products and services in the market. They soon discover that what little they knew about the last-mile operations was primarily theoretical. They also realize that offering a similar service to what is already available at lower prices cannot be successful. So, to accomplish that, they decide to burn whatever little cash they have to "make the numbers" with the discounted prices.

Now, they start to feel the heat of reality melting the positivity out of their perception. The founders are now making the slow but painful transition to Informed Pessimism. They are learning the hard way!

In the summer of 2016, I met with this brilliant entrepreneur inventor during one of my training workshops. He approached me during the lunch break and asked if we could chat about his startup. "I am into recycling. Do you know the large cardboard core of large printing press paper? I collect it and use it to make environmentally friendly lampposts. I invented a new process to harden the cardboard cores of large printing press rolling paper. I cover them with a special material mix on top of it and shape it into a pipe-like form using the machine that I also invented." He had this really proud look on his face as he took out this slight pipe-like shape and asked me to break it into halves if I could. I smiled and checked the pipe and found it to be substantial. As I examined it further, I could clearly see the cardboard and the carefully layered materials on top of it, making a perfectly shaped pipe. I asked him to share more about the end product – the lampposts.

"I use this process to produce highly durable street lampposts," he said. "It is not affected by rust and very cheap to install, maintain, and completely change if need be." He looked at me with a more serious face and said, "After I produce the main pipe, I add a solar-powered LED lamp to it. This makes my lamppost very easy to install because it doesn't need any electrical cables prior to installation and it makes it 100% more environmentally friendly."

He then complained about how potential customers like contractors and gated communities couldn't see the value of his product despite being a cheaper and more durable alternative to existing lampposts. He made some sales, but it was not enough to grow his small workshop, build up an inventory of cardboard rolls, and increase production. He tried to raise funds, but investors were not interested. They said they couldn't see the product-market fit.

This is an example of the typical mindset Preset Type 1 leaving the Uninformed Optimism state of mind and diving into Informed Pessimism.

This entrepreneur, although very smart, was not looking at things from a holistic perspective. He was not looking at value for the customer and by the customer. Like many entrepreneurs of Type 1, he was looking at what he could do or build. And he was very proud of it. I'll admit that he did invent something he should be proud of, but that's all. An interesting invention – nothing more; nothing less. *Basically, his startup logic was: "I invented*

something new. I think the benefit is great. I will now build it and sell it."
That is logic born in a vacuum and the direct result is a company on the
verge of bankruptcy.

In the fall of 2016, I met with a really inspiring entrepreneur. I remember how
he was straight to the point when we started our mentoring session. "As a
planet, we have a garbage crisis," he said. "I want to solve that."

He showed me pictures from all over the world with streets full of garbage and
how he wanted to change that. He invented a smart garbage box with a built-
in compressor to collect plastic bottles and soft drink cans, and the ability to
contain more than the regular garbage boxes.

"As people put plastics and tin in, the smart boxes will compact it to
maximize capacity. It will also automatically sort the garbage by type. When
full, the box will signal the nearest pickup team. The team will empty the box
and reset the system. They will then take the garbage directly to resellers and
sell it."

He finished his "pitch" with, ***"I think this idea can offer excellent value to the
planet. It can also be profitable with enough smart garbage boxes."***

"That sounds like a great tech," I said. "I can see your passion and your
hard work developing this system. However, I do not see any value for the
customer. What will drive regular people walking in the street to use your
box instead of throwing bottles and cans in the street or any other ordinary
garbage box? That is a big assumption from your side. You are taking their
behavior and motivation for granted."

"But it is offering great value to the planet and people should help preserve
the planet's future," he replied.

"If there is no value for the customer, there is no value from the customer," I replied.

"What do you mean by that? " He asked.

"If you look around the world, people care more about what happens today, in the now. Otherwise, we wouldn't have pollution or the garbage crisis in the first place. *They have to be motivated to actually use your garbage boxes. So what if we turn the bottles and cans into a currency?"*
"What do you mean by that?"

"Let us take university students, for example. They need transportation to and from the university; they need to have a snack or a meal and find a way to relax between classes. What if your Smart garbage box can offer them promo codes for transportation, meals, or internet credit for their phones in return for tin cans and plastic bottles? So, being environmentally friendly means I will have a discounted UBER ride back home or a free cheeseburger from McDonald's and so on. For a student on a budget, that is a great value, and for any company, that will be a great way to directly reach customers and achieve CSR goals."

"That makes sense," he said. "It will require that I change the design of my garbage box, but I think it might work. I will test it at the university."

And here is what he did, he redesigned his box and made it look very inviting in terms of design and colors. He added very interactive software combined with a touch screen. He heightened the experience by adding the element of surprise: customers will not choose what their rewards are for the bottles and cans. Instead, they spin a digital wheel and get something different each time they insert a certain number of bottles or cans in what he now calls the "CanBank." The test went very well. Students actually had a lot of fun using the CanBank.

Looking deeper at this conversation, i*t went from discussing tech capabilities to appreciating customer value,* even if it didn't have anything to do with the environment and the garbage crisis. What we got at the end was what made all the difference.

Basically, his startup logic was: "Tech will make a difference. If I build it, they will use it". That is vacuum-born startup logic.

It made all the difference when it became about the value and how to use tech to make this value tangible to potential customers. So his value-born startup logic becomes: *"Tech will make value tangible to potential customers and that will help to save the world."*

Mentoring Notes

To really help these entrepreneurs, give them the time to release all that stubbornness steam out of their system first. Then allow them to reach a point where they need to come looking for support because, at this point, they start asking questions. Mostly, they're the wrong kind of questions, but, nevertheless, the mindset is finally ready to question everything it took for granted. When they come asking, "What am I doing wrong?" don't give them an answer. Instead, guide entrepreneurs to write down everything they have learned in the field about customers and the product. Then, ask them to put everything in two columns next to each other. What usually happens is that they observe that they have so much information about the product and its features but relatively very little information about the customer's point of view. This exercise has proven very useful and helpful with Type 1 entrepreneurs. They write it down and learn from their own experience. Then encourage them to make it a habit. This process can become an excellent moment for many epiphanies.

If, on the other hand, you're aware that you possess this mindset or perception preset, take these mentoring notes and apply them to yourself in a form of self-mentorship. This will help you determine where you are on your journey.

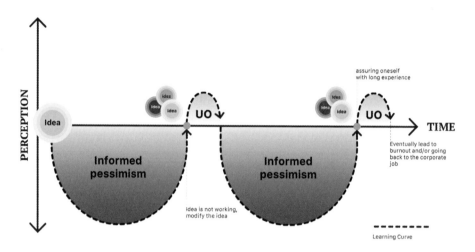

PERCEPTION

Idea

idea
idea idea

UO

Informed
pessimism

idea is not working,
modify the idea

assuring oneself
with long experience

Idea
idea idea

UO

TIME

Eventually lead to
burnout and/or going
back to the corporate
job

Informed
pessimism

Learning Curve

Figure 7: Typical Cycle of Learning Initiated By Perception Preset Type 1

So, what do we know from this now?

We know that this perception preset seems to be a prerequisite to a prolonged Informed Pessimism mindset state. Entrepreneurs spend so much time earning new experiences the hard way that they tend to iterate and change a lot in their ideas, mainly to reassure themselves and appeal to potential investors. They have very brief Uninformed Optimism periods, induced primarily by tiny victories, a potentially dazzling pivot, or by assuring themselves with their long experience in previous projects or corporate jobs.

This cycle of learning can quickly become a loop, enslaving entrepreneurs to backbreaking work and painful progress, if any. They keep putting in long hours, fewer breaks, and minimum self- care. Entrepreneurs keep doing this until they reach a certain level of isolation. They have minimum social activities or interactions with people outside the startup context. In extreme cases, the startup transforms from a passion to an obsession. The entrepreneurs become so fixated on making any kind of progress that they actually forget to eat, sleep, or even take a bath. This isolation can strain the entrepreneurs' relationship with family members, spouses, and friends.

If this loop continues to take place, entrepreneurs will pour even more hard work into the startup **until one of three things happens:**

- They will burn out and get out of the game,

- They will seek their old corporate jobs, or,

- They will end up offering freelance services.

They will hit the invisible wall of the mindset journey. It is like a fast race car pushing the brakes in the middle of a race at maximum speed. It is a harsh wake-up call from doing the same thing over and over again and expecting different results. It will inspire the entrepreneur to question their confidence in what they know for sure, and leave room for questions.

Perception Preset Type 2

BASED ON WHAT ENTREPRENEURS THINK THEY KNOW, THEY SEEK WHAT THEY THINK THEY SHOULD KNOW.

This type of perception preset is kind of popular as well. Many entrepreneurs who start their journey with this preset come from diverse educational backgrounds. They are not really in the startup for the sake of the startup. They are more in it for the sake of belonging to something bigger than themselves. They are usually relatively young and still define many things about their lives on top of everything they need to define for their startup. They typically start with confidence in what they think they know and progress quickly to mimic what they think they should know. In other words, they focus on the superficial and forget about the substance.

Yes, they are exploring, but they are investigating the dazzling society of entrepreneurship rather than the grinding world of building a startup. They're usually solopreneurs and, if they do have co-founders, they typically treat them as employees and not entirely as partners. In most observed cases, that co- founder leaves after a series of unfortunate conversations and situations.

These entrepreneurs quickly embrace the everyday slang of the startup community. They attend all the events, webinars, and keynotes. They read popular books and post about them on social media. They apply to competitions, incubators, and accelerators to get this sense of validation for their idea and themselves. After all, what could be a better validation of all their hard work than having the logos of famous incubators, connected accelerators, and challenging-to-win competitions right next to their startup name on their pitch deck? So they spend a lot of time applying, submitting, and using the hashtag #proud when they get accepted. They seek to meet with mentors, famed entrepreneurs, and ecosystem figures to validate themselves. Nothing is really about the startup.

In the fall of 2019, I met with a tourism startup founder who fell into this preset. She was considering a pivot by selling and home-delivering fresh vegetables and fruits online. I asked the entrepreneur whether she regarded her customers' perspective in this matter. *"Why would they buy fresh vegetables and fruits from a tourism startup instead of their regular providers?"* I asked. She replied that she had a fabulous new idea for a rebranding and showed me a logo. "This is not a pivot", I said, "this is a brand-new startup!" She continued talking about it, insisting that this was just a pivot and *that everyone was doing it.*

This startup has already been operational for more than a year and has raised some funds from a local angel investor. They have already graduated from two different incubation/acceleration programs. The founder has avidly spoken at many events about using tech to bring local tourism into the 21st century and, despite all that, the startup wasn't making any real progress. Her current startup was no longer attractive enough to make the headlines. Hence, she decided that the next step is to pivot to a more investor-friendly startup idea.

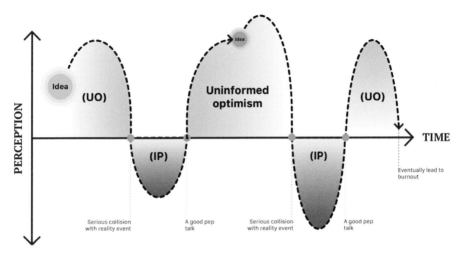

Figure 8: Typical Cycle of Learning Initiated By Perception Preset Type 2

This perception preset seems to be a prerequisite to a relatively shorter Uninformed Optimism mindset, closely followed by a smooth slide into Uninformed Pessimism. Because entrepreneurs are not learning much in this process, they are not making progress. This situation encourages many founders to start faking it until they make it. They want to make sure that they still fit within the accepted criteria of their environment and that their persona has not been damaged. In other words, they prioritize persona over startup. The deeper they slide into the Uninformed Pessimism mindset state, the more they resort to desperate "fitting in by faking it" measures. For example, they start manipulating the numbers, making big unattainable promises on social media, and overspending on digital marketing to give the illusion of growth and success. Not to mention that they are always "hiring" on Linkedin.

They enter a loop of really fast and continuously intensifying transitions from positive to negative unrealistic interpretations of the world. It is a loop of continuous collisions between their own perception of reality with what is actual and real.

This loop will keep repeating until eventually, one of four things will happen:

- The entrepreneurs will find a new idea relatable somehow to what they were trying to do, so they will happily embrace it and declare it a "pivot." In this case, the entrepreneurs move back to Uniformed Optimism. Armed with new material and immense enthusiasm, they seek to win competitions, get accepted into acceleration programs, and return to the social media spotlight. Uniformed Optimism is prolonged as much as the "pivot" will keep glowing under the limelight.

- The entrepreneurs get a good pep-talk from someone they consider as a source of "inspiration" (someone defined as important in the community). They believe the pep talk is a sign to push forward with the idea. In this case, the entrepreneurs return to Uniformed Optimism for a relatively short period before their mindsets fall to Uninformed Pessimism.

- The entrepreneurs fall deeply into the Uniformed Pessimism mindset and ultimately burn out.

- A combination of Points 1 and 2; ending almost certainly with Point 3.

I often observe that, at the height of the negative curve of Uninformed Pessimism, most entrepreneurs will completely stop what they are doing and reconsider their options. They reach a point where the startup is no longer attracting enough limelight. So, some become online entrepreneurship influencers while others will give "entrepreneurship" training. Many will seek to work with a famed startup as an experienced entrepreneur. Unfortunately, some entrepreneurs will be in need of support and perhaps some professional help to move on and find their well-being.

Perception Preset Type 3

BASED ON WHAT ENTREPRENEURS THINK THEY KNOW, THEY SEEK WHAT THEY THINK THEY DON'T KNOW.

This mindset preset is observed in the field predominantly among entrepreneurs with scientific backgrounds (chemistry, biology, environmental sciences), housewives resuming their careers with a passion project, and activists building their social startups. Passion is the hallmark of this kind of entrepreneur. They want to make a dent in the world and consider the startup as the tool to communicate and implement that change. This project is so close to their hearts.

Due to the fact that they mostly don't have any prior management or business experience, these entrepreneurs focus so much on what they think they don't know. Because of that initial deep feeling that there is so much they don't know, they are constantly worried. They begin with a relatively short Uninformed Optimism period and go directly to the Informed Pessimism mindset state. The mindset state is quickly embraced and for an extended period relatively longer than any of the other types. No matter how much work they put into the startup, for some reason, they go through phases of self-doubt and guilt trips. A rhythm of two steps forward and ten steps backward can be expected.

Type 3 entrepreneurs are solopreneurs who seek reliable co-founders. They begin the journey by themselves but always want to share it with a real partner. They have high expectations of their potential co-founders, so they can get disappointed easily in the people they choose to work with and change co-founders quite often.

In the summer of 2018, I started mentoring a chemist attempting to build a natural, organic beauty products startup. In our first session, I asked him why he was here. He shared with me that he was worried about his competition!

Then he started a 30- minute monologue full of specific details about two of them. According to him, his competitors were powerful. They were well funded, imported their own raw materials, and customers knew them well. They had substantial availability in all the vital online and offline stores.

I asked him to share more about his startup. He had not yet begun to build his startup but had only tested some product samples with random customers he met through his Facebook page. Initially, customers were happy to use his products, especially an all-natural facial cream. But he was worried about everything he didn't have and that the competition had. He felt overwhelmed and wanted to meet someone who could confirm his concerns and tell him what to do next. I asked him to share more about his current situation. He was already in the process of putting together a production laboratory where he wanted to produce around 1000 boxes a month of a new facial cream he had developed. He had also hired one assistant and an intern to help him with the production. He used his Facebook page to promote the products and answer any questions. He also displayed his products and met customers in local one-day bazaars. He was always searching for reliable suppliers and made sure to maintain a good relationship with them.

He stopped talking when I smiled and asked why I was smiling. I told him that he had enough to go forward. The real question that he should ask himself was whether the market needed another brand like him or not. He answered with a big yes, citing that more and more customers tend to buy from local brands because it is cheaper and more organic than anything else in the market. The market is definitely growing.

He was doing an excellent job for the current stage the startup was in. Comparing his progress with an already established business made him always doubt his efforts and look for what he didn't know or have.

"You need to learn how to size and segment your market and how to create a good distribution channel to reach more customers," I said to him. *"That is*

all that you need in the current phase".

"And my competition?" He asked.

"If the market is growing at the pace you describe, you should not worry about them. You should learn from them – from their mistakes. Build on them and move forward. Focus on what you have and do the best with it – as long as you can see a good and potentially rewarding opportunity out there in the market."

Yet another example of Perception Preset Type 3 came during the spring of 2021. I met this exciting team from Upper Egypt. They were working on recycling used denim into affordable baby clothes. Because babies grow fast, they change in size quicker than the parents can buy clothes. It becomes costly and wasteful as well. So, they decided to recycle fabrics from used garments to create nice baby outfits for different ages and at affordable prices. When I met with the entrepreneurs, they discussed accounting challenges, marketing, and funding. When I asked them about their validation activities, they replied that they didn't have any. They said that it sounded like a logical and great idea. So I challenged them. "Before the end of the workshop, ask five parents if they would buy clothes made out of recycled fabrics for their newborn babies." To their surprise, none of the parents felt they needed it since they had the clothes from the first baby already available. So they then decided to talk to first-time parents.

They managed to talk to another five parents. Fathers found the idea financially sound, yet the mothers found the idea absurd. "It is my first baby," one mother told them. "The first must get all the best, as it is our tradition. The second baby will just be borrowing from his brother or his sister," she continued.

When they returned to me with the answers, they were very disappointed. As we talked about it further, I managed to show them that what they have found out now will lead them to iterate but not completely change the idea. What they discovered at this point was much more important than accounting, marketing, and funding. ***They now know that customer culture and moms' points of view can have more weight on the final decision-making than the cost or the recycled fabrics.*** By the end of the workshop, they decided to target a different customer segment for their product. *They found that they could offer a profitable renting service to local NGOs supporting new mothers.*

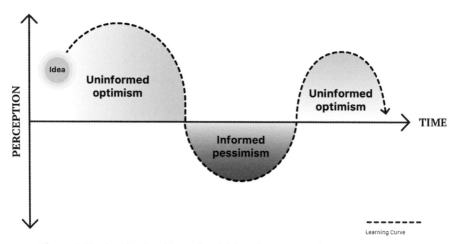

Figure 9: Typical Cycle of Learning Initiated By Perception Preset Type 3

This perception preset seems to be a prerequisite to a relatively long period of Uninformed Optimism followed by a rather long period of Informed Pessimism. As Type 3 entrepreneurs progress forward, the Informed Pessimism mindset states tend to be longer, and the Uniformed Optimism mindset states tend to get shorter and shorter.

Because some of these entrepreneurs really care about the dream – sometimes more than they realize it – they tend to take longer to accomplish the smaller steps. They zigzag a lot between going full steam ahead and completely retreating. Because they worry a lot, they put themselves under unnecessary pressure, thus, driving themselves deeper into Informed Pessimism.

This cycle of learning feels like a countdown towards the startup shutting down unless they are motivated to conquer themselves first. Type 3 founders can achieve so much once they can apply everything they learn from the field and use it to make progress on their journey.

With the invisible power of perception clearly ironed out, I would like you to use the Mindset Journey Kit in the following chapter before moving on to your startup journey.

"

With the right mindset, we can't lose. We either practice what we've learned or we learn what we need to practice.

Noura

06
The Mindset Journey Kit

It's important to think with these canvases now. They will give you insight into your own perception of yourself. But most importantly, it will help you align your perception with cofounders, and your founding team. Use the Entrepreneur Journey Map (EMJ Map) to reflect and align with yourself. The Actionable Vision Canvas is designed to help you align your perception with your cofounders. Finally, the Team Mission Canvas is about alignment with the founding team.

Ultimately, this is the trifecta that you need to be concerned with going forward. Of course, the customers are of importance, but that is not related to your mindset journey. That is related to your startup journey and, as I've already mentioned, you and your startup are not one.

Now, let's focus on the Entrepreneur Mindset Journey Map (EMJ).

The Entrepreneur Mindset Journey Map

Throughout my journey as a mentor, I developed some exercises and tools to help my entrepreneurs navigate their mindset journey. I also learned a couple of things from them as well. This chapter is dedicated to share with you some of them with you.

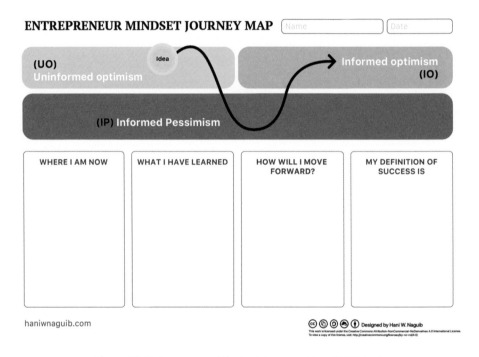

Figure 10: Entrepreneur Mindset Journey Map (EMJ Map)

This tool is designed to help the entrepreneur stop, reflect, and understand the fast-paced journey. It is also designed to be used multiple times with the purpose of comparing notes each time it is used. By discovering the differences and the progress in the journey, the entrepreneur is capable of appreciating the journey and its effects on a more meaningful level. As this learning process continues, the entrepreneur is capable of reaching the third phase of the mindset journey, informed optimism, much faster.

How to use the tool

1 - Where I am now

- Use dates and/or time frames to map the most memorable events that took place since you got your startup idea. Use table 1 to guide you.

- With each event, write down the most memorable emotions you can remember.

- Use the key characteristics of each phase as a guide.

2 - What Have I learned

- Once your position on the EMJ map is clear, consider the key learnings you have accumulated throughout the journey.

> ### *Use the following statement to answer this question*
>
> During_____(phase), the most important challenge I met was_____
> (challenge), I dealt with it by_____(actions) and this led to_____
> (consequence). The lesson I learned was_____
> _____.
>
> **Use simple terms and take your time to reflect on it.**

3 - How will I move forward

- Now that you know where you are, how you feel, and what you have learned, it is time to move forward. Leverage your learnings into actions.

Use the following statement to answer this question

Based on _____(learning), I will _____ (action) so that I can accomplish _____(potential outcome).

Use action verbs and think of the results of those actions.

4 - My definition of success is

- Defining success must be tangible and specific. Think about what could be the best metric to measure a successful completion of your moving forward actions.

Use the following statement to answer this question

I will know that I am successful when _____(identify your main criteria for success) happens, and_____(key measure) is satisfied.

Putting it into practice

Setting   Choose a quiet place with a big wall.

Tools   Pen, sticky notes, and a large print of the canvas (A0), hang it on the wall.

Type   Personal exercise.

When   At least once every 2 weeks and for as long as you think you should document and learn from your journey.

Exercise Steps:

1. Start by identifying where you are on the curve in the EMJ map.

2. Trace back all the key events and people, and so on that, you think led you to where you are now. Place them on the EMJ map.

3. Reflect on your journey and write down all the key learnings so far.

4. Digest your learnings and think about how you will use them to move forward with your journey. Use Action Verbs.

5. Give a metric to your actions to be able to measure your progress. The metric could be time, number of hours/days, and so on. Remember, a metric is something you can measure and quantify clearly.

Actionable Vision Canvas

The Actionable Vision Canvas is designed to connect your personal mindset progress with your startup progress. Once you reflect on your journey and its learnings, it is time to harness all that to the benefit of your Startup Journey. Use this tool to communicate and align the vision with your co-founder(s). Make sure that it is about the big picture. In other words, use the canvas to include not only your learnings and aspirations but also the learnings and aspirations of your co-founder(s).

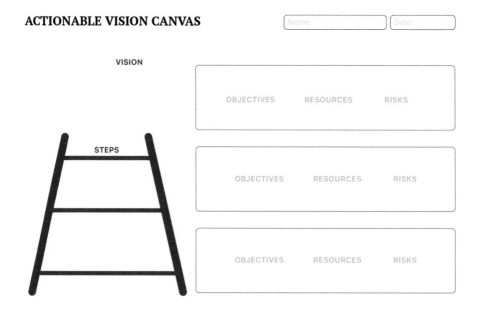

Figure 11: Actionable Vision Canvas

How to use the tool

1- Vision

- Ask yourself, "Where will my startup be in five years?" Make sure to be concise and clear with your wording.

2- Steps

- What are the main steps that you need to accomplish in order to reach your short-term vision? Keep in mind that every step leads to the next. In other words, each will build on the other units until you are able to accomplish your vision.

3 - Objectives

- Write down a list of all the objectives needed for a successful accomplishment of the step(s).

4 - Resources

- Consider all the resources that you must have in order to accomplish your objectives.

5 - Risks

- Consider all the risks that you could possibly encounter while attempting to accomplish your objectives and how they might affect your team, your progress, and the startup as a whole.

Putting it into practice

Setting Choose a quiet place with a big wall.

Tools Pen, sticky notes, and a large print of the canvas (A0), hang it on the wall.

Type Personal exercise or with your co-founder(s).

When At least once every four weeks and for as long as you think you should.

Exercise Steps:

1. Start by identifying where you see your company in five years. Write it down in simple terms. Make it tangible and measurable.

2. Now, break down this vision into three main steps.

3. Identify the main objective, the key resources needed, and the risks associated with each step.

4. Once you are done, give each step an assumed time frame for completion and decide on who is step leader or the person responsible for monitoring the progress of each step.

Just as this canvas can be used to assess where you are on your journey and where you would like to be, you must also take stock of this from a funding standpoint.

Team Mission Canvas

Your mindset isn't the only one of importance on this journey and that is where this canvas comes in. The Team Mission Canvas is designed to help you align your startup's big picture with your team. You want to learn about the mindset of your founding team and make sure that it is heard as well as included in the realization of the big picture.

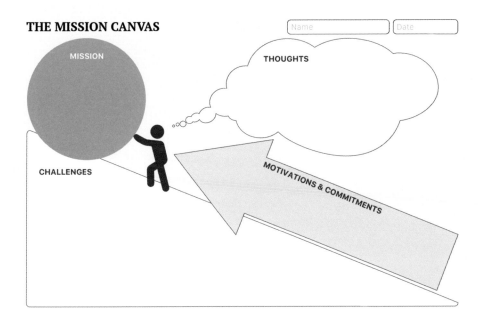

Figure 12: Team Mission Canvas

How to use the tool

1 - Mission

- Compile the objectives from the Actionable Vision Canvas into an executable mission. Make sure to highlight the importance of each. Open the discussion for the team's input into the subject.

2 - Challenges

- What are the main steps that you need to accomplish in order to reach your short-term vision? Keep in mind that every step leads to the next. In other words, each will build on the other units until you are able to accomplish your vision.

3 - Thoughts

- Now, ask your team to express their thoughts about the mission and the challenges. Make sure they feel safe enough to express themselves. You don't want a "yes" team.

4 - Motivations & Commitments

- You must understand the team's motivations to accomplish the mission. Make sure to include everyone in the discussion.

This section will be a startup culture formation guideline for you and your co-founders.

Exercise Steps:

1. Start by communicating the mission (remember the objectives in the Actionable Vision Canvas?) to the team. Ask why they are here, and what they need to accomplish together.

2. State the challenges and risks (remember the risks in the Actionable Vision Canvas?)

3. Now it is time to include your team:
   - Give them some time to include their thoughts about the challenges and mission presented to them.- If not, then what changed?
   - Give them time to include their motivations (and concerns) about the challenges ahead, and to display their commitment with action verbs.

4. Now that you have all communicated your thoughts, mindsets should be clear about the path and what needs to be done. Happy hunting!

NOW THAT YOU FULLY UNDERSTAND THE IMPORTANCE OF YOUR MINDSET, WE CAN SET OUR SIGHTS ON THE ACTUAL STARTUP JOURNEY.

2

The Startup
Journey

"

The journey is the reward.

Asian Expression

07
Delving Into The Startup Journey

As mentioned, you've now reached the point where your mindset journey has become clearer to you. We can now walk the road of the startup journey together and you will begin to see just what I mean by this being a braided journey. We begin this leg with an understanding of how entrepreneurs view their own startup journeys.

When I ask early-stage entrepreneurs about their startup journey, most of them share how they got the idea, how they started developing it, or what they had to go through to raise funds.

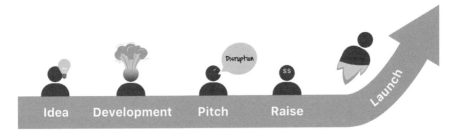

Figure 13: The Misconceived Startup Journey Process

In a way, most entrepreneurs described what they were doing in a linear format as seen above. They would give an inventory of the steps they followed. However, this wasn't the only thing I noticed. There was also their own tone of voice while they were sharing the story. This would reveal if they were proud, happy, disappointed, or angry. It felt like their own evaluation of their performance up until that point of the journey. In most cases, they were way harsher than they should have been.

A repeating observation from my conversations with entrepreneurs is how they emphasize how different their startup idea is. They really stress what they consider crucial differences. However, when I gently push back and help them dig deeper, they usually land somewhere along the lines of, "It will be better, cheaper, and faster than the competition." You have no idea how many times I have heard this sentence and, every time I do, I can clearly see the impact of the "it must be different at all costs" culture on founders, especially the novice ones.

If, by any chance, you are thinking in the same manner, please ignore those thoughts. *You can never offer a better and cheaper product at a faster speed – and definitely not all at the same time.* It also shows how you don't really appreciate your customer, market, or competition. If you think that your customers will only want what you offer because it is sold at a lower price, you really have nothing substantial to show them and should reconsider your whole startup idea.

This is another repeating observation from the field and it's actually my favorite one: when asked about their potential customer segments, most entrepreneurs rush into describing them by class A, B, C, or D. They deem this alphabetic system enough to represent customers and rationalize why they decided to target them in the first place. For some reason, they all seem to want to target class A or B. This unwritten consensus is that customers in classes A and B earn more and can afford to buy and pay more. Therefore, they are the best customer segments to target. I have no idea how this view was formulated or why it was popularized. Still, it is not just the Egyptian entrepreneurs who embraced it. In several conversations I had with other mentors from Europe, Canada, and the UAE, they mentioned similar views embraced by their local entrepreneurs.

Another interesting observation is how entrepreneurs believe that building a business-to-business (B2B) model would be less complex and cheaper to implement than a business-to-customer (B2C) model. They feel that working with small and medium enterprises (SME) or corporate customers can be less challenging than setting up operations to interact with households and individual customers. I don't know how this generalization came to life! However, it is definitely gaining momentum and is often applied as a real business shortcut.

Your focus as a founder should not be solely on the customer segment but rather on the value proposition within the context of the customer segment. Hence, the kind of infrastructure your business needs will depend significantly on the value proposition and how it should be offered to the targeted customer segment in a profitable and reliable way.

Another key observation from the field is how personal the startup journey can become for most entrepreneurs. On several occasions, I observed the startup becoming a manifestation of the entrepreneurs' hopes and dreams. For example, I hear sentences like:

"When my startup is successful, I will finally get married to my fiancée."

"When my startup is successful, I will prove to my family that I was right to leave my job."

"When my startup is successful, I will be set for life."

All these thoughts are valid, but they add too much weight to the shoulders of the young and "still learning to walk" infant that is your startup. Building a startup is more about the startup and less about the entrepreneur behind it. Building a startup is about what that startup needs to blossom. What the entrepreneur needs to get out of the startup is a potential outcome of what the startup needs. Think about it this way. If you are growing a tree to sit in its shade, it will require the same amount of time, resources, effort, and care as growing any typical tree. Adding more water, and fertilizer, or exposing it to more sunlight will not make it grow any faster. In fact, it might end up killing it.

Growing a tree is not about you. It is about the tree itself. You will have to familiarize yourself with all of the science behind it. You will do research, talk to other tree growers, find experts in the field, and try to provide everything the tree might need to blossom and prosper. When the tree finally does blossom and flourish, you will be able to enjoy its shade, fruit, and beauty. But most importantly, the tree will become the undeniable monument to all your hard work and diligence for all to see.

You must always consider the startup's point of view as if it were a living being and, accordingly, as an entrepreneur, you need to continuously upgrade your capability and skillset to meet the challenges along the way.

Getting married, becoming successful, proving yourself right, or being set for life are some of the results that a thriving startup can offer you as a founder. But this all has nothing to do with the startup itself. Focus on your startup's needs and your startup will eventually take care of you.

In the summer of 2020, I was approached by a young entrepreneur seeking to build a fintech startup focused on a "buy now pay later" value proposition. She reached out because she was frustrated that she could not convince any investor to support her and hoped I could help her understand why.

She did some research about this type of startup but, still, she had barely scratched the surface of the inner workings of the business model. Her approach was not innovative and she did not have any experience in relation to the field. When I asked her why she chose the "buy now, pay later" model, she replied with a long ungraspable monologue. Then I changed my question and asked her, what do you hope to get from this startup? She instantly replied: "Independence from my family and respect when I am successful." The contrast in the clarity of both answers was interesting. When I asked her about the startup, the answer was long, hesitant, and really not clear. But when I asked about her motivations to build a startup, her response was intimately and spontaneously about her. Not only that but it was expressed in a crystal clear and organized manner.

As a mentor, this is a tough-love moment!

"Your startup will not be able to get you the respect you crave unless you focus on the startup's best interests. Right now, the startup is nothing more than a hopeful catalyst to achieve your personal goals. Those same goals can be achieved if you land a corporate job. You don't need the startup for that! Your startup is a living and breathing entity that needs care, especially in its infancy. If you wish to continue working on your startup, you should understand your business model better. Focus mainly on its key resources, your potential customers, and how they approach and deal with the concept of debt. You should also consider your legitimacy as a founder of a fintech startup. Understand how investors, and the fintech community, evaluate the fintech founder. From my perspective, you will gain much more by working for an already established fintech before you actually build your own."

She promised to consider all of my advice and get back to me later with her action plan. On that note, we concluded our session. Needless to say, I never heard from her again. However, a few weeks after our conversation, I learned that she has decided to "pivot" to build an NFT-based art-focused startup.

This is not uncommon in the startup journey for many would-be founders.

So, what is a startup journey?

The startup journey is the faith-based, conscious decision to explore the potential value of an idea. It is a journey of transformation, where a diligent entrepreneur transforms an idea of value from its abstract form into a tangible entity that can potentially create value sustainably for a specific customer in a profitable and growing manner. The journey needs to be focused on learning about everything a startup needs in order to become a competing and thriving reality.

In other words, ***the startup journey's ultimate purpose is for any entrepreneur to become value-literate!***

The purpose of the startup itself is to become a profitable and competing company – a fact many entrepreneurs seem to forget about while taking a "growth at all costs" approach. Growth is good, but too much growth can be devastating as well. It is like asking a one-year-old to have the personality of a 25-year-old just so as not to disappoint the in-laws. Of course, the in-laws here are a referral to the investors.

In the past few years, I have witnessed the primary interest in creating a startup shift from building a profitable business to nurturing a well-sponsored growth machine. Startups were no longer offering value for the customer and receiving value from them. They simply became growth machines; well-fed with investors' money and not by the sales made from real customers.

High-growth machines built on the large fires that are fed by burning investors' funding look good in the media. They can serve as a great social media accomplishment. However, this type of venture eventually dies with the last burned bag of cash. How long they survive depends entirely on the fundraising skills of the entrepreneur.

A startup is a temporary machine used to discover value for the customer and for the business (from the customer). It is all about customer value at this stage. Investor value should come at a later stage. Think of it this way, investor value is a by-product of achieving customer value. You will never achieve investor value by forcing customers to buy your products. Promo codes are just temporary fixes. They are not magic. Once the value is validated and implemented, a startup needs to transform into a company to survive the competition.

Mentoring Notes

Common founder blind spots at this stage are:

Confusing a charismatic startup CEO for a potentially profitable business model! Many founders think they can charm their way to profitability/ funding.

- Confusing awesome PR/marketing for an equally awesome value proposition.
- Confusing raised funds for potential success with customers.
- Confusing one positive survey for value proposition validation.

Just as founders have to go through cycles of learning where their mindsets are concerned, they also need to go through levels of learning maturity with regard to the startup itself.

The Startup Journey's Four Levels Of Learning Maturity

When I look at the startup journey of any entrepreneur, I am really not talking about steps on a linear timeline. I am talking about startup levels of maturity that are reached every time entrepreneurs can achieve a specific degree of understanding of value. Every time they attain that understanding, they move forward to the next level with different elements to discover, organize, and adapt to within their startup. Moving from one level to the other depends significantly on the entrepreneurs. Progress is not bound by a specific duration and most definitely varies depending on every entrepreneur's personal capability.

One of the commonly observed challenges to many entrepreneurs on their startup journey is personal financial security. In our ecosystem, funding in the early stage is not as available as it should be. Many founders, especially those with families to support, work full-time jobs while performing their early idea validation work.

One of the entrepreneurs I briefly mentored was driving his car as an Uber to make enough money for himself and his family. He also used his driving time to chat with some of his clients who fit the profile of his potential customers. Despite the fact that he could not focus on his startup full-time, he managed to find a way to make money and work on his startup's validation work. Another entrepreneur gave private math lessons to high school students while building his startup. He managed to stay on top of the cool trends by having conversations with his students and applying them to his trendy youth-focused startup.

You see, the startup journey is not made from the typical linear steps on a timeline as some might consider it to be. Instead, it is an ongoing exploration, moving forward with enough resilience to accept that it will sometimes be necessary to go back to an earlier level and re-explore what was once considered well- defined. That is why the journey of building a startup is iterative and nonlinear because we have to continuously iterate our understanding of value as we progress forward on the journey.

On the startup journey, there are four main levels of learning maturity:

1. Idea

2. Idea Startup

3. Piloting Startup

4. Scaling Startup

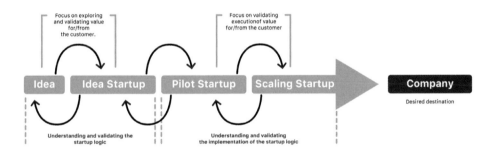

Figure 14: The Startup Journey's Four Levels Of Learning Maturity

These four levels should eventually lead to the startup's transformation into a company. In other words, all your exploration and validation activities fulfilled their purpose and have reached their destination: the clear-cut day-to-day execution of a validated & profitable value for the customer and value from the customer. Your understanding of value has reached maturity!

In many cases, this journey can and will lead you to understand that your "idea of value" is not of any value from your customer's perspective or the perspective of your business – or both. That is why I encourage founders to go through the first level by finding ways to thoroughly evaluate the potential.

These four levels should eventually lead to the startup's transformation into a company. In other words, all your exploration and validation activities fulfilled their purpose and have reached their destination: the clear-cut day-to-day execution of a validated & profitable value for the customer and value from the customer. Your understanding of value has reached maturity!

In many cases, this journey can and will lead you to understand that your "idea of value" is not of any value from your customer's perspective or the perspective of your business – or both. That is why I encourage founders to go through the first level by finding ways to thoroughly evaluate the potential value of their ideas with the least time, effort, and money possible.

Following this approach will also offer you the opportunity to be value-focused throughout your startup journey while making progress with evidence. The power of evidence is that it elevates your discussion with potential investors from relative, sometimes opposing, opinions to tangible insights based on which they would be more than willing to put money in.

Another benefit of this approach is that it replaces the focus of building products with materializing value using technology. You move from building fintech, agri-tech, prop-tech, and whatever other industry-focused tech, to developing value- tech. In other words, you are creating a startup that offers value materialized with technology. Eventually, you only build products and services that you have undeniable proof of value for.

Finally, this approach helps see your startup as an engine of value and not just an engine of growth. It shifts your attention from building something that has short-term appeal to potential investors into a company that can produce long-term customer value.

Startups are engines of value.

Now, let's see how this is learned.

Learning Level 1: Idea

When you are at the idea level, your natural intuition will drive you to consider how it can be different to ensure that your startup has an edge. You will consider this edge as your primary defense against those who will criticize it. The more the criticism, the more time, effort, and even money you will spend to make this edge look as glamorous as possible. You will even focus on being different from anything possibly thrown at you, especially any companies that might be offering something similar to your idea.

But what you don't realize is that being different doesn't necessarily ensure an edge and being different for the sake of being different is just a waste of resources.

In the summer of 2020, during a mentoring session, one entrepreneur enthusiastically shared with me how he wanted to create a dessert-only ordering platform. He kept talking about how the online experience would make all the difference and that he would handpick the menus based on top quality and best prices. He even had fantastic branding ideas. I have no doubt about this wonderful entrepreneur's passion for his work. It was undeniable in the way he presented his arguments. But in this case, the idea had progressed in his imagination really fast. But, remember, it wasn't the business opportunity that he was talking about! He was totally in love with his idea. When you seek to evaluate the opportunity, you need to consider your idea within a context. An idea is nothing more than an abstract notion of value. It needs to be focused on a value proposition within the context of other similar value propositions in a specific market. At this stage, you need to understand how similar you are *first* before you start talking about differences or edges.

Mentoring Notes

Ideas come with alluring promises and seductive potential. They embody everything that can be possible when it is successful. And potential success brings with it all these endless possibilities of a better tomorrow. In a way, an idea becomes associated with hope. So, be careful when you are discussing an idea with an entrepreneur, especially first-timers or really young entrepreneurs. You are probably discussing "hope" with them and not just a business idea. Instead of criticizing the idea, make sure to guide them to see the blind spots in their logic. They will respect you for it. Remind them that when they have an idea, it must reflect an opportunity that can be profitable and sustainably grow. So, instead of wasting time developing arguments to defend the idea, like the "my idea is different" argument, they should spend time understanding the business opportunity behind the idea.

So, this is what I asked him to do.

I asked him to conduct similarity research.

Similarity Research

The purpose of similarity research is to find the proper context for your idea and evaluate it in contrast to that context.

First, you need to focus the idea on a value proposition to a specific customer segment. A common mistake is assigning multiple customer segments for the same value proposition. This is confusing and usually a waste of time. Focus on one potential customer for one value proposition. If the idea includes more than one customer segment, like in the case of a marketplace, then make sure that each of them has the corresponding unique value proposition. Ask yourself this: What kind of benefit am I offering to my customers? What kind of costs am I helping them avoid? Value is nothing more than the difference between benefits and costs from the perspective of the person receiving it. And yes, benefits and costs are not just monetary and tangible. They can be emotional and completely intangible. Human beings aren't simple creatures and how they perceive value should be given the proper depth.

For example, consider a newly engaged young man taking his in-laws to dinner for the first time. Having a credit card with him at this moment is not just a tool to pay for that dinner. A credit card would be, at this point, a safety net for the young man – something that will help him avoid embarrassment in front of his new family in case the cash on him is not sufficient to pay for the check. A credit card represents emotional safety at a critical moment for that young man.

Another common mistake is found in the way that many entrepreneurs confuse products or services with value propositions. That is a common phenomenon I often see in the field. Products and services are nothing more than the interface and experience through which a customer can receive value. You will use technology to accomplish that, *so technology is not value in itself. Instead, it is a medium through which customers can interact with value.*

Once you have defined your value proposition to a specific customer, you will need to consider the kind of technology necessary to materialize it into a product or service. In other words, can you use already available hardware/software to fit your needs? If not, can you modify the existing hardware/software? If not, do you need to invent something completely new to make your value proposition a reality in your customer's hands?

Once you have some answers, the next step would be to consider a simple comparison with other value propositions and tech needs in the market. You want to understand how similar your thoughts of value were to what is already there and how technology was used to materialize it. Start with the market in which you intend to launch and then expand your research worldwide. Find failed examples as well as successful ones. If the examples you find in the market are those of already well-established companies, research them at their early stage. Focus on how they got the idea and developed it into a value proposition. Then, find out how they materialized it into a product or service using tech. Use all this research to help you see the blind spots in your logic.

The primary purpose of similarity research is to appreciate the big picture from different perspectives.

What can you learn from the value proposition similarity?

Learning about similar value propositions can tell you whether you are contemplating offering an already existing value proposition, a modified version of an existing one, or a completely new one. This information will shape your decision to go forward with the idea, pivot from it, or forget about it with the least cost possible (time, effort, and money).

And what would that tell you?

In The Case Of An Existing Value Proposition

When the value proposition is almost 100% similar to other value propositions in your targeted market,
you are most probably entering an existing market with:

1. Existing customer segments,

2. Defined business models,

3. A known value chain, and,

4. Stakeholders.

A bit of good research can go a long way. It can help you understand whether this market is on the rise, plateauing, or in decline. It can also tell you a lot about the level of competition in that market and whether there is room to enter or not.

For example, consider the dessert ordering platform. This is a very similar idea to typical food aggregators, only it is more specific to desserts. Most entrepreneurs will focus on the dessert part as a differentiation of the idea. However, their obsession with being different doesn't allow them to see that the idea is more similar than different. At the end of the day, it is about the traffic on the site, the home delivery process and speed, and the marketing budget. Being just for dessert might make it more difficult than easy. Most customers already have accounts on existing websites that deliver both savory and sweet foods.

Modified Existing Value Proposition

When the value proposition already exists but with some variation, you are probably entering an existing market with existing customer segments. However, because your idea has some variations, you should not limit your research to the market, business models, value chain, and stakeholders. You need to spend time understanding how happy those existing customers are with the value propositions already available in the market. You will determine if there is an opportunity for your idea by understanding if your potential customers are looking for a better version of the existing value propositions. In other words, the opportunity will be in the possibility of re-segmenting the existing market and catering to its needs.

In the summer of 2020, I had a conversation with an alternative-meat startup founder. He was having a hard time promoting his 100% vegetarian meat to restaurants and chefs. He was seeking to understand how he could sell more. It had the same taste, same texture, and exactly the same smell he shared with me. He was frustrated that he could not sell enough of what was considered an excellent product. I told him that selling vegetarian meat to meat-eaters doesn't make sense. At the end of the day, you are trying to convince people to replace something they know with what is perceived as a replica of the original. You need to point out that your vegetarian meat is the diet cola to Coca-Cola. It is good protein but without all the unhealthy characteristics of red meat. You will be addressing a segment of an existing market of meat lovers who are conscious about their health and would be very happy to find a healthier option. So, your value proposition is not about being vegetarian but being healthy while still enjoying eating meat. You are now addressing a re-segmented market.

New Value Proposition

When the value proposition is unique, and there is nothing like it in the market, you are probably in the process of creating a new market. This means that nothing is yet defined and your targeted customer segments are unknown. In that kind of venture, you are in the uncertain realm of innovation. You are perhaps in the most challenging area of entrepreneurship and it is not for the faint of heart. The question is, how can you put your idea within the context of other value propositions out there if there is nothing to compare it with?

Well, don't think about it in this way. Instead, appreciate that your value proposition either offers a new solution to an existing problem or tackles a new and rising problem or opportunity. For example, consider Uber, the ride-sharing platform. It provides a new solution to an existing problem: easy access to transportation options based on budget, occasion, and/or distance.

Now, let us consider Virgin Galactic, the American spaceflight company founded by the pioneering entrepreneur, Sir Richard Branson. It is seizing the opportunity to be the first to market offers of commercial suborbital spaceflights to space tourists. Uber is thus compared to other modes of transportation, while Virgin Galactic could be compared to other high-adrenaline sports and experiences. Uber had offered the world the freedom to move with a click of a button. Virgin Galactic offered adventurous customers the next unparalleled thrill.

What can you learn from the "tech needs" similarity?

Using Existing Tech

Tech needs are the kind of technology you will need to materialize your value proposition into a product or service. The value proposition will either use existing hardware/software, modify existing hardware/software, or invent completely new hardware/ software. So how can that help you?

In the case of using existing hardware/software, your primary focus will be on the user interface (UI) and user experience (UX) aspects of the development. Everything you need is probably already available and can be realized by third parties or hired consultants and freelancers. Customers will be used to the technology and have some usability, durability, and price expectations.

This information will guide you to consider the market sizing and to target the market share you want to go for in the first three to five years of your startup. Accordingly, you can determine what kind of sales and marketing strategies you need to develop. Finally, you will be able to formulate a budget to reach that market share.

Using Modified Existing Tech

In the case of modifying existing hardware/software, your primary focus will be on finding the right talents for your technical team. Unlike the existing tech case, your product or service probably relies heavily on the technology. You will need to have a talented Chief Tech Officer (CTO) early on as a co-founder. It will also mean that you will probably have some patents/trade secrets in your company's name. That is usually good for the company's valuation, competitiveness, and potential existing strategy, especially if you have something that big companies might want to get their hands on. So, make sure to have a good patent lawyer as an advisor early on.

Customers will be more or less used to the technology aspect of your product or service. However, you will probably need to make sure they understand the difference in your modified tech instead of what already exists in the market. Think of Apple when they explained their M1 processor during its introduction keynote. Most people didn't necessarily understand the technical details but comprehended how M1 represented an advantage for them. The M1 processor in their phones, tablets, and computers meant they could do a lot more at a faster speed, thus, using less battery power. With the M1 processor, Apple managed to deliver an existing value proposition using better tech.

Using New Tech

Finally, the new hardware/software needs to materialize the value proposition into a product or service. You should expect that you will need a tech team and infrastructure early on. Your tech becomes a critical component of the startup and must be developed in-house or with the help of really reliable partners.

A talented CTO becomes an indispensable part of your journey, so, make sure that you have the right mind and character on board with you from day one.

You should also consider that your customers will most probably need to have this technology introduced to them in a way that will make sense to them. Think of Apple introducing the first iPhone. Steve Jobs introduced the tech in a familiar way to potential customers. He showed them step by step how they could easily use the iPhone to do more than the available phones at the time. I encourage you to watch the 2007 Apple keynote where he first introduced the iPhone. It will give you a good sense of how to pitch your value proposition.

Defining Similarity

This is perhaps one of the most confusing parts of the process. How can you define which companies you should compare your value proposition with? Well, that is the keyword here: value proposition, not product or service. In other words, we are not talking about features. We are talking about end-result benefits and costs from the perspective of the potential customers.

For example, what do you compare Red Bull with? Other soft drinks? Other energy drinks? Red Bull is not a soft drink and nothing like it existed when it was first introduced to the market. People were using Red Bull to stay energized – to keep doing what they were doing longer. Whether it was for partying at clubs, studying for finals, working out at the gym, or spending a late night at the office to finish that client presentation on time, it was always about having enough energy to keep doing a specific activity. The same thing can be achieved with an espresso, green tea, caffeine pills, or a Snickers bar. It all depends on the customers' perspective of value within a specific context. Let us take an example that I heard from a friend of mine while he was doing his residency in a local hospital. Medical students prefer green tea when studying. However, they will go for a Red Bull during a busy shift at the emergency room. Green tea will help them study without the jitters that accompany the use of too much caffeine. At the same time, Red Bull will keep them energetic during a busy shift at the hospital without needing several coffee runs and the subsequent frequent bathroom breaks.

So when you are defining similarity, think from the customer's point of view or perspective. Think customer benefits and costs. Factor in the emotional dimension and not just the tangible or monetary ones. Use these parameters as your main criteria to choose the proper context for your value proposition context.

Finally, once you have identified the similarity factors for comparison, make sure to research all the similar value propositions out there, including the ones that were not successful. ***Make sure to look at both the failed and successful ones.*** There is so much you can learn from that.

Exploring Value In The Field

In the context of entrepreneurship, what is the difference between research, validation, and testing activities? This is a common vocabulary calibration that I like founders to appreciate to ease our communications during the mentoring sessions.

Research Activities

Within the context of entrepreneurship, research activities are conducted when founders are seeking to learn from already available information. Their hypothesis of value is already proven and much can be learned easily from the previous experiences of other founders, industry reports, and market forecasts.

This is advisable when you have an existing/modified value proposition and existing/modified tech needs.

Validation Activities

Within the context of entrepreneurship, validation activities are conducted when founders are seeking to learn and cannot find any substantial data or information with typical research activities. Their hypothesis of value has not yet been entirely proven and lacks evidence. They conduct experiments to collect data and find answers.

This is advisable when you have a modified/new value proposition.

Testing Activities

Within the context of entrepreneurship, testing activities are conducted when founders are seeking to learn about the functionality and reliability of the tech needed to materialize their value proposition. These testing activities range from the development of a proof of concept to the creation of a final product (proof of concept + UI/UX).

This is advisable when you have modified/new tech needs.

The Startup Value Stack

The Startup Value Stack, which is your road map for the idea startup learning phase of the startup journey. It is not a linear process. It is an iterative approach to understanding value one question at a time.

You have 4 main simple questions to answer:

1. What are the benefits and costs from the customer perspective? Are the benefits higher than the costs? And that is value for the customer.

2. What are the benefits and costs from the business perspective? Are the benefits higher than the costs? And that is the value from the customer's perspective.

3. Is the proof of concept technically doing everything it is supposed to be doing? And that is tech proof of concept.

4. Can the customer get the value when/by using the product or service? Is the experience, the interface, the design, and the interactions all aligned to deliver that well-validated value proposition to the customers? And that is the product or tech with user experience and interface on top of it.

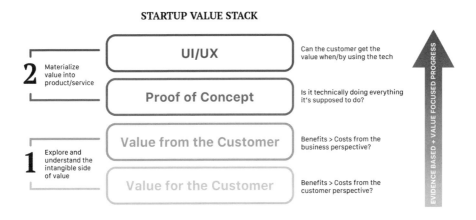

Figure 15: The Startup Value Stack

Those are perhaps the most critical questions you will need to have good answers to and suitable proof before talking to any investors. You will be harming your chances with investors if you approach them without sound evidence of what you have to say. One small note on validation activities, you are not seeking to find out what is popular and go with it. You seek to understand what is essential for people who can be your potential customers. You will then design and create to offer the customers something that positively impacts their lives. Validation is not a search for consensus or your way of advertising your product or service early on. Most certainly, it is not about you or the investors. Validation activities are about learning the most you can about value from different perspectives with the least effort, cost, and time possible.

Remember, *you only move forward when you have learned enough about those four perspectives.* However, you will achieve results because of how you implement those learnings in the field. Essentially, the Value Startup Stack emphasizes an evidence- backed understanding of value before engaging with investors.

Learning Level 2: Idea Startup

This is the second level of learning on your startup journey, in which you make your first actual step towards becoming a value-literate entrepreneur.

The nature of value can be exceptionally confusing for many people because it is both intangible and tangible. In other words, value can be perceived with emotions and logic. A credit card can help you buy things you can't afford today for your children. So, in this case, a credit card is a tool that enables your role as a "good" father and provider (intangible) and the ability to buy now and pay later (tangible).

Another example, to the untrained eye, Uber can be seen as a mode of transportation that takes you from point A to B. Well, that is the very tangible, logical way of looking at the value proposition of Uber. But we are human beings and it is not just about logic. If you take a deeper look at it, Uber actually offers you the freedom to move at any given moment. So having the Uber app on your smartphone is the equivalent of having "freedom" in your pocket. If your car breaks down, Uber can take you to find help. If you have an argument with your fiancée and have no car, calling an Uber can liberate you from prolonging that tense situation.

And this is an intangible and emotional way of seeing value for the customers.

The formula for value is quite simple:

$$\textbf{Value} = \textbf{Benefits - Costs} \text{ [13]}$$

But to really appreciate value, you must understand it from your customers' logical perspectives as well as their emotional perspectives. So if the value is equivalent to benefits (emotional/ monetary) minus the costs (emotional/

financial), you will need to understand how the customers define them. Then, you will need to discover when this equation results in a positive outcome (benefits>costs).

And from that, you can define the value *for* the customers.

In the context of a startup, value is a two-way stream. Think about it this way: If you want to offer value to your customers, you must receive value back from them. That is the critical balance of any startup. When this balance is not sustainable and scalable, we don't have a real business – only a temporary project with a limited shelf life. As you dedicate time to understanding value from the perspective of your customers, you must spend an equivalent amount of time understanding what kind of value your business needs to receive from your customers. You are seeking to quantify value for the customers in terms of a price the customers are willing to pay and in a way that the customer will be happy to do it with. That quantification must offer your business the means to strive and compete (benefits > costs) sustainably.

But that is not all. You also need to understand whether there is something else you need from your customers other than money in return for a purchase. For example, in the case of a social media platform, you actually need your customers to be comfortable enough that they are willing to offer you their data. You also want them to be happy enough that they are willing to help you bring more people onto the platform and become your positive word-of-mouth ambassadors.

Value from the customer is not only about the willingness to pay. Sometimes, it is also about the willingness to share, support, or contribute.
And from that, you can define value from the customers.

Once your value exploration has yielded a positive outcome, it is time to consider how you can best materialize value into a product or service. To materialize value, you need to develop the "ugly prototype" or the engineering proof of concept first. I call it ugly because the primary focus of the prototype is functionality and not how it looks. This is basically what your technology must be able to do to deliver the discovered value. In essence, this is engineering from the perspective of engineering. Once you have accomplished that, you have proof that it works. Don't be too eager to make it perfect; not just yet. You need just enough evidence that it can function correctly.

That should be followed by engineering from the perspective of the customers. In other words, you should start exploring how your customer would use this technology intuitively and reliably.

Of course, you are now thinking of UI/UX and considering all the A/B testing, fake buttons, paper low-fidelity prototypes, and wireframing possibilities for your app, website, and so on. You are right to some extent. However, I am actually thinking of something less tech and more human. For example, in the case of a ride- hailing app for motorcycles, your potential customers will sit in close proximity to the motorcycle driver. In this case, the use of deodorant becomes a top priority for a pleasant customer experience.

So, yes, in this case, the proof of concept should be focused on writing the needed code for the ride-hailing app that allows customers to interact with drivers. However, the interface and experience would need to expand from app-human to human- human. So don't limit your work to wireframing. Talk to your potential customers and see how you can define the experience and the interface in this case.

Another example is if you are building an e-commerce website. It is not only about the shopping experience online, but it is also about delivering the purchased product and the interaction with customers, including feedback loops, customer service in case of product returns, and refunding procedures. So it is not just the website-human component. There is also the human-human interaction that must be considered.

Remember, your aim is not a finished product or service yet. ***You are rather focused on an exploration of value materialization.*** It is a learning process and not an implementation procedure. So keep everything at low fidelity.

Idea Startup: The Kit

Customer Progress Canvas

Throughout the startup journey part of the book, I have spoken of – and will continue to speak of – value and the jobs-to-be-done approach to understanding customer value. The customer progress canvas is a tool created specifically to help founders understand value from the customer perspective using jobs to be done [14]. The theory of jobs to be done states that when customers realize that there is something better out there for them within a specific context of a situation they are in. That creates a dynamic view of the customer and the way they define value. In the NOW state, how the customer defines value (NOW value = benefits - costs) has become less desirable in contrast with the appearance of better alternatives, or the TO BE state. Hence, the creation of a new and different definition of value (TO BE value = new benefits - new costs). Putting those definitions side by side proposes the highlight of the customer perception of progress.

The gap between those two definitions of value creates a vacant job. The question becomes, what can the customer buy to help them move from the less desirable NOW state to the more favorable TO BE state? The answer would be in all the possible products and services out there that allow the smoothest possible transition from the NOW state to the TO BE state.

CUSTOMER PROGRESS CANVAS | Project | Date | Version |

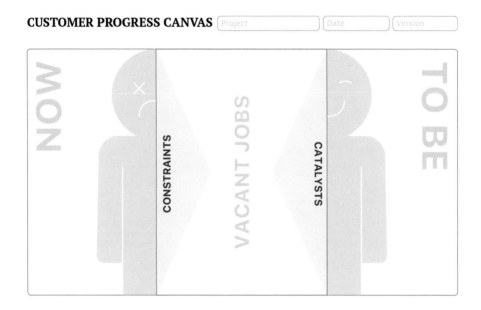

Figure 16: Customer Progress Canvas

The three levels of design thinking empathy are often used by the founders I work with to define value in the NOW and TO BE states.

The three levels of human-centric, design-led empathy [15]:

① *What are the customers doing?* Conduct observation sessions in the field to observe potential customers in real-life situations. Remember to observe your customer in their natural habitat as much as you can. It is important to observe them in their day-to-day life.

② *What are the customers experiencing?* Find a suitable, with no potential danger to yourself, to immerse yourself in what the customer is experiencing.

③ *What are the customers saying?* Based on everything you learned from the observations and immersion session, design and conduct customer interviews to give more context to those prior learnings. Your main purpose is listening and reflecting with customers on how they define value in both contexts (NOW-TO BE).

How to use the tool

1 - The NOW State

- Using a design thinking approach to empathize with customers, make sure to describe (in their own words) actions, stories-based insights, feelings, and the emotions deduced. From that, define the NOW benefits and costs. Make sure to define the outcome (the NOW value) in a way that can clearly showcase that customers are not really satisfied with the current state.

2 - The TO BE State

- Follows the same approach as laid out in Step 1 but with a focus on appreciating the possible definitions of more desirable TO BE benefits and TO BE costs. Make sure to define the outcome (the TO BE value) in a way that can clearly showcase that better outcome for customers.

3A - The Constraints

- Based on everything you witnessed during the three steps of design thinking of empathy, you want to describe all of the possible constraints that are challenging your customers or preventing them from making the move from the NOW to the TO BE state. Remember, the constraints can be emotional, social, and functional.

3B - The Catalysts

- Based on everything you witnessed during the three steps of design thinking of empathy, you want to describe in this section of the canvas all the possible catalysts that can help smooth the transition from the NOW to the TO BE state. Remember, *the catalysts can be emotional, social, and functional.*

- At this point, you have defined the challenge/the problem that your potential customer is facing very well. You have put the two definitions of value in contrast to each other and provided a context for them using the constraints and catalysts.

3C - The Vacant Job

- Now comes the most interesting part of the canvas, which was left empty until the very end for a reason. Once you have the right and left side of the canvas populated with enough insights, ask yourself this: What kind of product/service features can be hired/bought by the customer to overcome already explored constraints and respect predefined catalysts to make the smoothest possible transition between the NOW and TO BE states?

- Highlight the features quickly without commenting on them. Once you have them, make sure to translate them into a very low-fidelity prototype and seek out customers' perspectives.

- Now is when you can think of your products and services as tools of value used by your customers to make progress. Please note that, up until now, tech was not mentioned at all. Tech will come at a later stage. This tool will help you answer the first question in the value exploration stack on the value for the customer.

Pro Tips

- Make sure to always differentiate the assumptions from the facts. I tell founders to use orange sticky notes for the assumptions and blue for the facts.

- When you highlight anything as a fact, make sure to have a sticky note behind it with the key reference that proves it is a fact. Without a strong reference, it is not a fact and at best it is a well-rounded assumption.

- When you start the exercise, make sure to cover the whole of part 3 of the canvas with a blank paper. Make sure to focus only on the customer NOW and TO BE states – nothing more; nothing less. Remove the blank paper once you feel that you have completed the first two parts and have enough information to tackle the third part. If you feel that you haven't covered everything, then ask questions about what you think is missing and that you must know. At this point, you either go back to your notes and dig deeper, or go out and run the three levels of empathy again with more focus on what you think is missing.

Learning Level 3: Piloting Startup

Congratulations! You have reached a new level of learning. At this level, you need to learn how to be a manager and a leader on top of being an explorative and passionately curious entrepreneur. With applied curiosity, you have asked questions and found answers. You are value-literate, meaning that your idea of value has taken shape and form. But now, you must get ready to become value- execution literate! Your concept of value needs to have the right infrastructure to successfully materialize the validated value proposition to a scaling and competitive product or service.

This level of learning is called the Piloting Startup Level. You will explore, understand, and validate the best ways for your idea of value to reach your customer in a tangible and profitable form. This also means that you will need to build the proper infrastructure and test it on a small scale to learn, modify, and apply the best possible outcomes. It is also a great way to get your newly hired team to work together and go quickly through the Tuckman's [16] forming, storming, norming, and performing scenarios.

The question is, what kind of infrastructure does a startup really need? If your answer is resources, money, offices, computers, talents, and so on, you are probably right but not entirely. You see, these are all components of infrastructure. However, without the right set of processes or the written rules and the right culture or the unwritten rules, they remain components. Your processes and culture create the suitable glue that gives these components shape and meaning. They guide founders to make the best choices possible to continuously balance customers' best interests with the business's best interests. They also serve as the leading guidelines for your employees to make the best choices possible to continuously balance their best interest with the best interest of the business and the customers.

For some time now, you have been working with a small group of people on validating your startup idea. In other words, it was people performing activities. And that was good enough for the needs of the previous levels of learning.

But now, it is not!

Now your challenge is to figure out how to transform those activities into repeatable processes and how to make all of those interactions between people the seed for good, nurturing, and responsible culture. To accomplish that, you need to consider many new elements, perhaps for the first time.

Building the Infrastructure: The Processes

When you begin to work on the process, start with the value proposition and the customer. Ask yourself this: What are the most critical activities you constantly need to perform well to make the value proposition available and tangible to your customers? These are the key activities that you must absolutely own and control. Now consider all of the supporting activities for your key activities to initiate and perform well. Those can be handled by third parties and are not essential to own at this phase of your startup. You need them, but you don't need to own them because they don't contribute directly towards realizing your value proposition to your customer segment.

In the summer of 2019, I worked with a unique tech startup. They were one of the very few startups in my hometown that used relatively advanced tech to materialize their value proposition. They used augmented reality technology to create virtual showrooms where clients can interact with a whole range of products in just two square meters using advanced virtual reality (VR) and augmented reality (AR) tech that they had developed themselves. They targeted customers in the car retail, jewelry, and furniture businesses. They offered them the opportunity to spend less on rented space and the ability to expand faster in terms of vital geographic locations and a number of showrooms.

When the founders talked about building their company, the most critical key activities on their list were B2B sales and constant software development. But they kind of missed the fact that to accomplish what they were working towards, they needed to perform technical talent acquisition exceptionally well. Without getting talented and professional software programmers and finding sales specialists with both excellent market knowledge and software sales experience, the startup would never be able to achieve its plans. And those became the key activities.

But then come the roles of the supporting activities, such as contract drafting, hardware supplying, and tech support. They need them to complement the work of the key activities. However, they are not that critical to owning or operating at this startup phase. It is much more efficient to find third-party entities to fill those activities on their behalf.

Building the Infrastructure: The Culture

In the first two learning phases of the startup journey, you were exploring an idea of value. It was you, your co-founders, and a few founding team members. Life was simple then. You had your traditions as well: ring a bell when you land a big customer, go out for dinner when you reach a milestone, have a show-and-tell once a week with a small breakfast, stock a large fridge with your favorites drinks, and conduct an in-office ping-pong tournament to encourage healthy competition.

That is not culture, by the way!

Remember when an employee made a mistake and got punished for not coming to you, the founder, to ask for permission? That is culture.

Remember when you got sushi for everyone when they achieved targets on time? That is culture.

Remember when you dismissed the words of an employee in a meeting with a client? That is culture.

Remember when your customer complained about your after-sales service and you made fun of them behind closed doors? That is culture.

Remember when you landed that big account and you didn't recognize the sales team/person behind it? That is culture.

Culture is the sum of small moments where a human being feels the difference between being included or dismissed; the sense of being appreciated for contributing and being churned; the feeling of empathy by colleagues versus sympathy. Culture is not something tangible. It is not what you write down in a "culture manual" and distribute it to all employees. People will not read it and, if they do, they will probably only use what echoes their own beliefs and principles. *You begin from the beliefs and principles that your value proposition needs to exist within to strive.* If it needs to be customer-centric, you need employees who would appreciate listening to other human beings around them. Your value proposition will be best served by having a personal and direct customer relationship offered by friendly employees capable of patience.

What defines a culture is what is being rewarded, what is being punished, and how this is all being done. Accordingly, it will explain what are considered positive and negative attributes in a potential employee. Dynamic and attractive founders usually contribute very much to the definition of the startup culture from an early stage and, without knowing it, they can quickly turn their culture into that of a cult. Basically, they will be hiring or firing people according to their own perspective of what is positive or negative. Hence people will take cues on what is right and what is wrong.

As a founder, you don't need to form a cult at your company. The first person harmed by something like that would be you! You will be surrounded by "yes" men and women all the time. And you really don't want that!

What you punish, what you reward, and how it is communicated to the team needs to serve your startup's value proposition to the customer segment.

In the fall of 2018, I worked with two charming founders. They were intelligent, dedicated, and kind-hearted. They had just finished their validation work and managed to raise some funding to establish operations. I went to visit them at their new office. During my visit, I witnessed something interesting. One of the founders conversed with an early hire on the startup founding team. Here is how the conversation went:

The founder: "Have you managed to follow up with the client list I shared on Slack?"

The team member: "Not yet. I will get right to it."

The founder: "OK, I will wait for your feedback on the progress."

The founder then joined us in the open space, where his co- founder and I sat and chatted.

Five minutes later, the team member asked the founder if she could leave the office. She said she had something else to do. The founder replied with a yes, of course.

He looked at me and said he was trying to build a relaxed culture around the office. "So why is your employee asking for permission to leave the office?" I responded. Without waiting for his response, I asked him whether the newly hired employee completed tasks on time. He responded with a "no". The early hired employee was actually lacking in the area. He went on to say, "She hasn't been at the office much for the past month and is behind on most tasks." Then he started this 15-minute monologue about the difficulty in finding good-caliber employees and how they are doing their best to be understanding.

"At this relatively early stage of your startup journey," I said, *"your employees will take cues from what you punish and reward.* If you are okay with them leaving every time they ask or having relaxed deadlines, it will become the usual thing. You are creating a norm where the customer's best interests are not being served by not rewarding a better follow-up behavior. If you are not convinced or if you don't care about something, your team will feel it and act according to this feeling. And, yes, if someone on the team is acting as if they are too good to abide by the culture's rules, they must be let go immediately and without a second thought. If you let them stay, you accept the behavior, which is a signal for the rest of the team to say it is okay to be like them."

One last challenge for this stage: hiring!

Two primary quotes I find founders using often:

1. *"Hire for Attitude and Train for Skill"* was originally attributed to Herb Kelleher, one of the founders of Southwest Airlines. Although it is a great and correct quote, it doesn't apply in the case of a startup at this stage. Perhaps it makes perfect sense in the context of hiring in an established company with an existing and experienced human resources department as well as learning and development departments. However, in the case of a startup at the piloting stage, you need to have the right attitude and the right set of skills. Don't compromise on that.

2. *"Hire Slow and Fire Fast"* Founders talk a lot about taking their time in hiring someone new while not thinking twice when it comes to firing. This process can be efficient if you have enough time, resources, and talented people to handle your hiring activities. At this stage of your startup, you will probably have nothing of that sort. Instead, consider investing in building a selection process that is linked to a well-defined culture.

Hiring your first team is one of the most thrilling and definitive moments on your startup journey. Find people who will challenge you and those who will complement you. Don't look for the comfort of the "YES" employees. Find curious minds who are seeking to find answers. Hiring your first team speaks volumes about you as a founder. Who you hire first will showcase your priorities, your personality, and your mindset state.

Usually, founders finish the Idea Startup phase hungry for funding, restless to implement, and eager to watch the idea basking in the light of success. They bypass the Piloting Startup phase and rush into the Scaling Startup phase. They spend all of their time fundraising while making investor-attractive numbers happen. As they keep hiring new people and growing in size, geographic locations, and ambition, founders notice that the newly hired are not fully integrating, the relatively older employees are not performing, and many are leaving only after a short while.

So, many founders burn a lot of cash on standing desks, colorful bean bags, and branded extravagant welcome packages, thinking that they are creating an incredible and attractive culture. Because they haven't spent the time to build the proper infrastructure of their startup (the right culture and the right processes), they learn the hard way about the critical importance of piloting. It is like blowing up a poorly made balloon to its maximum capacity too quickly and aggressively. What do you expect will happen? Under the pressure of all that air, the balloon will begin to crack until it blows up in your face.

Yes, many founders ignore this stage until the harsh realities of the journey guide them directly back to it. At that moment, having enough funds left to do that turn-around is a different question completely.

Piloting Startup: The Kit

In the spring of 2019, I ran into a founder during an event. I hadn't seen him for some time. He is the type of entrepreneur who puts all his passion and energy into his work. He worked diligently on his product design and built a decent sales funnel in practically no time. His hard work quickly attracted renowned international investment powerhouses, investing six figures to expand the business further in the MENA (Middle East and North Africa) region. It was a great startup story, written with the hard work and diligence of this amazing solopreneur.

But that is not how the story ends. The founder was not his usual fun and calm self. He seemed different. I knew that because I had worked with him for almost four months during his time at a local incubator. We started chatting about life, the startup, and everything in between. I learned about the status of his company and how fast things were going. Since he received the investment, the team had doubled in a very short period of time and was based in two countries. He had some really good people, however, the turnarounds were really high. "The atmosphere at the company is not as it used to be," he emphasized.

Then he started talking about the numbers. He had hired an ex-Uber growth manager to ramp up the numbers to satisfy his investors. The guy did come through by consuming a lot of the cash on hand to acquire customers with what they discovered later on as very low lifetime value.

Ultimately, the startup was not in a good place and with a shorter runway than expected. He wanted to fix things but he didn't know where to begin.

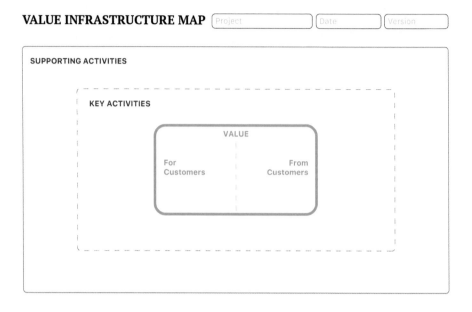

Figure 17: Value Infrastructure Map

That day, I drew this framework to pinpoint where he should start his reform of the startup.

I asked him to answer the following questions, and in this order:

1. What is the value proposition and how does it serve specific customers?

2. What are the most critical activities my team needs to perform in order to make that value proposition materialize to the targeted customers? (For example: product design, marketing, advertising, and pricing)

3. What are the most critical activities my team needs to perform in order to let the customers offer value in return or buy the products/services? (For example, sales activity, after-sales service, delivery options, product availability, and logistics).

④ What kind of supporting activities does my team (or third- party teams) need to do in order for the critical activities to perform well?

⑤ Finally, what kind of culture do I need to emphasize in order for the team to appreciate their roles, the value proposition, and the customers? How can I materialize that into something tangible?

I asked him to spend some time reflecting on these questions until he found some answers. They didn't have to be complete or perfect – just some initial thoughts.

Then, I asked that he go for the following approach:

① Add one senior employee from a core activity to the conversation by asking them to give the list of questions a try.

② Make a quick comparison of answers and highlight both the major differences and major similarities with the first set of answers.

③ Update the answers by including what makes the content more inclusive and insightful.

④ Add one relatively junior employee from a different core activity to the conversation, and offer them the questions to answer.

⑤ Repeat points 2 and 3.

⑥ Repeat point 4 by alternating between relatively senior and junior employees. Keep doing that, until the set of answers no longer needs any updates.

⑦ Now, group all of the people who joined the conversation. Throughout the new conversation, share the inclusive answers with them and highlight any misconceptions found in the answers.

⑧ Figure out, the best way to transform those insights into tangible accountable actions with them.

⑨ Finally, make sure that this approach doesn't take more than a working week to go through.

A couple of weeks later, I got a phone call from the founder with his feedback. He discovered that many of the newly hired employees had their own personal and professional interpretation of what the company was doing currently and should be doing next. The definition of the value proposition and its customer was vague to most people outside the product and marketing teams. The KPIs that were set during this phase were more focused on achieving the "now" numbers for the investors without minimum regard to reaching profitability or deeply understanding value from the perspective of the customer. Employees were leaving because of the absence of a clear chain of command, particularly when it came to suggestions and ideas. Finally, the active and talented employees didn't have a clear understanding of what they could and couldn't do.

The idea behind this exercise was not to get definitive answers but rather to ask better questions. By putting different perspectives of the business in context with each other, the founder was able to find some of the blind spots in his approach. But then, by putting the perspective of the newly hired versus the ones who had been in the company since the start in contrast with each other, he was able to find even more blind spots in his approach.

Working with the team, hand in hand, he would be able to make the business better and create a sense of ownership by including the team as well.

And that was his starting point toward piloting.

Learning Level 4: Scaling Startup

The startup journey has a very interesting relationship between focus and interactions-based politics. As commonly observed, the more you progress on the journey, the more your focus shifts from customers to investors.

At each level of the learning maturity, depending on the level of startup politics, founders can find themselves shifting their focus from customers to investors and losing money, precious time, and overall value in the process.

This phenomenon usually intensifies at the fourth and final level of learning maturity of your startup journey. *At this level, your aim is to understand how best to scale your culture and processes in order to be able to deliver your value proposition to an increasing number of customers,* and possibly in multiple markets, while making sure you are progressing steadily towards profitability.

However straightforward this might sound to you, it is much easier said than done. Believe it or not, the challenge in this phase is not in the actual understanding of how to scale your culture and operations. It is actually about doing so while you, as a founder, are being completely and unequivocally distracted by the maturing startup politics and the constant battle focusing on customers' versus investors' best interests.

The "Startup Politics"

As you grow in terms of your number of customers, you simultaneously grow in terms of the size of your operations and employees. At this point, the startup has been there for a while now, and culture is forming and evolving. As you have managed to raise funds and fill up the war chest with enough resources to last you for the next couple of years, employees begin to have a sense of calm security that replaces that overwhelming "fight for the startup" mode that they have been in for some time while trying to get

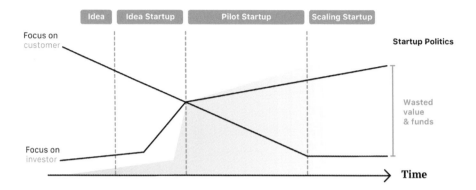

Figure 18: The Intersection of Startup Politics

the startup on its feet. Founding team members become somehow entitled and expect a special status and treatment within the increasing ranks of the team. Well-funded scaling startups represent a great opportunity for corporate employees who are seeking to advance in title and salary, and who are not capable of doing so inside their organization. They capitalize on founders' need to hire employees with presumably corporate experience to help them with their scaling efforts and promote confidence in the startup. Some investors see corporate employees at a senior level of the startup as a vote of confidence in their investments. That is why many founders seek to hire senior corporate employees on their teams. However, they seem to forget that newly hired people come with the culture of their previous jobs. In many cases, founders don't realize that they are actually contaminating their culture with another.

How can you define startup politics?

Startup politics are all the results of co-founder-co-founder interactions, co-founder-team interactions, and co-founder- investor interactions and that can impact the progress of the startup journey, positively or negatively. In most of the cases I witnessed, startup politics wasted precious time and funds.

In each of these types of interactions, and depending on the startup's Level of Learning Maturity, the level of politics increases, reaching perhaps its highest level at the fourth level. I want to share what I have learned from observing the same founders over long periods of their startup journey and the biggest challenges they went through.

The Customer-Focus vs the Investor-Focus Dilemma

I must admit, I never thought that the idea of focusing on the customer while you are growing your company could be that difficult to maintain. One would think that since founders have been focusing on customers for three learning maturity levels, it would be muscle memory to have customers front and center. But that is not necessarily true. At this level, as founders raise capital, they actually include VCs and angel investors, with their backgrounds, priorities, and of course their cultures, into the startup culture. ***Investors become more vivid and tangible than customers.*** If you think about it, at this point, customers are nothing more than numbers on Excel sheets, while investors are those very deep voices on the other side of that monthly follow-up call. They come with recommendations, guidelines, and, in some cases, intrusions on the final decision-making. Examples witnessed in the field range from pushing founders to hire expensive ex-corporate employees and Ivy League graduates to renting a really expensive office space and including well-known but non-compatible figures on the startup advisory board. One other key example is the nonstop push to make growth numbers at any cost. Focusing on your investor at this stage is like having an affair. You are losing the big picture and everything you worked hard for, just to have momentary, short-term satisfaction. You are losing touch with what matters the most: your customers. You are replacing income based on sales with income based on funding. Shifting focus from your customer to your investor means you are becoming a sponsored project with one big client: the investor. It also means that you are no longer the CEO of a startup. You have become a freelance project manager – there simply to pump up the valuation and dump it on the next round of investors.

The question is: Is there a way to manage your focus as a founder at this stage?

The answer is yes! You need to think of raising funds in a different way. Consider this formula when you think of funding:

Raising Funds = How you PR your evidence

The public relations (PR) component of the formula must be 100% investor-focused.

The evidence component of the formula must be 100% customer-focused.

It is not about what you tell your investors but, rather, how you tell it to them. It is about making the right impression about yourself using all of the evidence you have accumulated on your journey. It is not about altering the evidence to make the investors happy but rather **presenting your evidence in a way that aligns with the investor's investment thesis.**

Think of Hampton Creek [17], the maker of vegan products that is fighting hard to regain credibility after the company was caught rebuying its products from its distributors to pump up its sales volumes. The founders wanted to display higher market demand for their vegan mayo right before their Series C fundraising round. The founders were good at PR but compromised the evidence. That is usually a sign of a weak value for/from the customer. You can't grow the sales of something wanted by very few people.

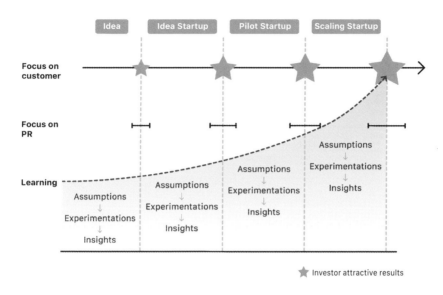

Figure 19: The Marriage Between PR and Evidence in Funding

Another very famous example is Theranos [18]. If you haven't heard of Theranos, then you have probably missed out on one of the biggest controversies in the world of startups. This health-tech startup was founded in 2003 and ceased operations in 2018. In its lifespan, it was able to raise over a billion dollars worth of funding to develop tech-based devices capable of running blood tests at a fraction of the blood volume usually needed. Of course, what the founder promised was not actually possible. Despite the fact that many renowned scientists and experts [19] actually announced that same fact, the founder was really great at PR and made the right impressions with the investors. It goes without saying that both the CEO and COO were charged with fraud.

I found that entrepreneurs with the best results in raising funds were usually the ones who were best at PR themselves. The thing is, as history shows us, raising funds is not the aim behind a startup, but rather just a stepping stone on the long journey of building something of value. Raising funds on its own doesn't guarantee success. It just betters the odds. Being able to do PR well, having good charisma, and having a great catchphrase for your startup can make all the difference in raising funds.

The founders who actually "make it" are those who take the time to define value, find enough evidence for it, and know how to communicate it in a way that the investors appreciate.

In a nutshell, your PR as a founder is basically about showcasing your startup logic (or evidence-based concept of value) in a way that appeals to the logic of your potential investors while making the best impression about yourself as a person and as a business leader.

I also noticed that the founders who had little funds to work with or "bootstrapped" were the ones most dedicated to their startup's progress. The delayed gratification, in this instance, can make the startup's progress align with the founder's progress – a place where the two areas of progress seem to intersect for a good period of time. This intersection harnesses the founder's focus on building up to a bigger finale.

Consider ZOHO, the startup that grew to become a $1 billion company without any VC backing [20]. The founders focused on building products that offer clear value to their customers and to their business. That balanced approach allowed ZOHO to grow but at a slower pace than the typical growth-at-all-cost approach.

At the end of the day, progressing through the four learning levels requires you to, eventually, come to the realization you're your customers should always be your top priority. Now, with the startup journey's four learning levels in mind, it's time to take stock of your progress before moving on to the actual practical applications within the realm of funding.

"

I've spent
my whole life
searching for
the impossible.
Never imagining
that I will be
the impossible.

The Flash

08
Startup Journey Progress

In this section of the book, I want to address perhaps the trickiest of questions: how can you know if you are making progress on your startup journey?

Progress on the startup journey is not only based on your accumulated learnings but also on how you use and implement such information to move forward and create momentum for your startup.

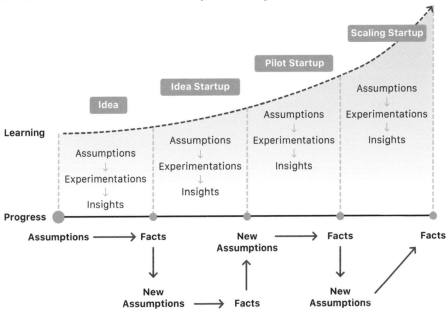

Figure 20: Startup Journey Progress

Lessons at Each Level of the Startup Journey

There is what you need to learn at each level of your startup journey and there is what you will do with it. These are two different things but, together, they make all the difference for any founder seeking to point a startup in the right direction.

When you start your journey, you literally begin with assumptions and very cool "what ifs". In my opinion, this is the equivalent of a very aesthetically pleasing but tasteless dessert! So you transform your assumptions into hypotheses and evaluate them with experiments in the real world to gain real insights. At a certain point, you are capable of accumulating enough insights that you can clearly make the distinction between what is fact and what is fiction. You keep working until you have enough facts to declare this level of learning maturity complete. You have enough facts to venture to the next level and build on it.As we discussed in previous chapters, each level of learning maturity has different parameters to explore and appreciate. However, at each level, you grow from the minimum to the maximum possible insights by moving from your business-related assumptions to insights. This process is very popular in entrepreneurship. It was introduced and perfected by Lean Startup practitioners. However, without context, this process can mislead you into experimenting for the sake of experimenting. In other words, putting in a lot of effort is mistaken for making progress. The learning maturity levels serve as your context – as your guide and direction towards a better understanding of what you need to know.

Assumptions, experiments, and insights are a process not a destination in itself. Yes, you need to learn how to structure your assumptions, coordinate your experiments, organize your results, and discover the key insights from your data. This is really crucial. However, without the right context, you are missing the point behind it all.

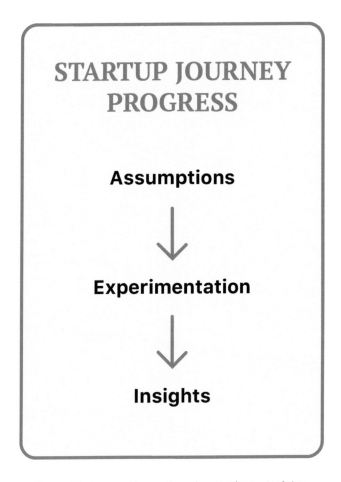

Figure 21: Assumptions - Experimentations - Insights

One of the biggest mistakes many entrepreneurs make is that they don't carefully and meticulously document their assumptions, experiments, results, and insights. And because of that, many end up duplicating experiments and efforts. The journey itself is about accumulating learnings at each level to maturity to build the next one on it. So, make sure that you spend enough time documenting everything in an organized and readable manner. It will serve you well when you meet with your potential investors for the first time. It will display your mindset, your efforts, and, most importantly, how you got to your evidence at each level of your journey.

Another common mistake is having many people responsible for one single experiment. The experiment ends up being led by comity! This is a compromised design to please everyone. Every single experiment you conduct should have a very clear person in charge and this should be the person with the last word. Everyone can contribute, but one person assumes the full responsibility and full focus on the experiment conducted in the field. Another common mistake is not having a common way of reporting results, especially at the early levels of learning maturity. It will cause confusion, especially at a later stage, if the person in charge has left the team for any reason. As you go forward with your experiments, make sure to continuously unify and update the way you report your experiment, results, and insights.

The next common mistake is not having a clear budget for your experiments. I find that adding such a constraint can be great for finding some of the most creative ways to discover what you need to learn about value.

One last common mistake is trying to learn too many things with the same experiment. If you are running experiments on your value for the customer, don't include the price in it. Price means you are testing value from the customer. If you don't have any real evidence behind value from the customer, then you should not try to quantify it with a price.

Once you have learned what you need to learn, you will use it to execute your business in real time. You are no longer a startup because you know enough to be able to create value for your customers and value from your customers with a reliable and sustainable approach. You are now the proud owner of a company and applying everything you have learned in order to manage the day-to-day operations, competing for market share and looking for the right moment to make the right exit.

Transforming assumptions into facts is perhaps one of the most rewarding yet consuming experiences you will ever encounter on your startup journey. It is rewarding because it will offer you the opportunity to examine all of your

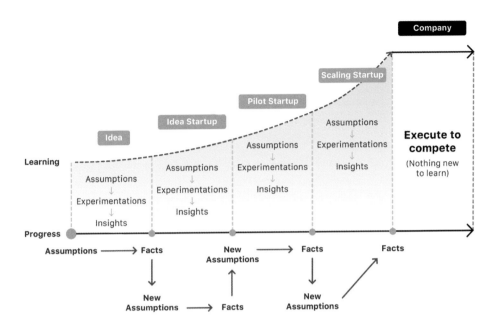

Figure 22: Exploring Value as a Startup & Execution as a Company

ideas, thoughts, and dreams in real time. It will teach you new things about yourself and what you are able to do, and it will most definitely surprise you a few times. It consumes your energy because you will be thinking about the experiment design, the significance of the data, and what kind of insights you can extract from it nonstop. You'll think about these things while you are in the shower, having lunch with your family, in a meeting with a potential client, and sometimes in your dreams.

Consider the case of Quibi, the startup that raised $1.8 Billion in total to offer millennials a mobile-only video streaming app that offered content in the form of 10-minute-or-less episodes and shut down only a few months after they launched [21]. It is basically a hybrid of Netflix and YouTube. The startup was backed by the likes of Disney, Alibaba, and Comcast alongside big names in the investment world. It was founded by two experienced founders, Jeffrey Katzenberg [22], Co-founder of Hollywood Pictures,

DreamWorks Pictures, and DreamWorks Animation, and the former CEO of Hewlett Packard Enterprise, Meg Whitman [23], who also acted as Quibi's Chief Executive Officer (CEO). Quibi had all the funding it would need, the experienced leadership and team, and the right support from gargantuan media companies like Disney and Comcast. But what they didn't have was the right value proposition – just the assumption of possible value for and from a potential customer segment. Here are some of the key critical assumptions **that Quibi never considered validating:**

- Will potential millennial customers find 10 minutes or less content appealing to watch on their phones?

- Since Quibi will use the content of third-party producers, will they provide good enough content for viewers to follow and be willing to pay for?

The founders of Quibi, formerly known as New TV, consciously made the decision that they would not do any kind of validation for these critical assumptions. They actually decided that "if they build it, customers will come" and went full steam ahead in developing the platform and the app [24]. The result was translated into almost 90% of the estimated five million customers who downloaded the app not signing up for a subscription beyond the free trial period [25].

In October 2020, just a few months after its launch, Quibi decided to shut down and return about $350 million to its shareholders [26]. The world of funding should not be any different from the world of building a startup: value-focused and evidence- based. It should give room for founders to explore value with minimum funding and, hence, minimum risk. If the exploration shows potential, then it should be allowed to continue further. Funding should go hand in hand with the quality of evidence found in real life. Funding should be offered to incentivize progress.

Evidence-based progress requires evidence-based funding. There, I said it.

"

Ideas are easy.
Implementation
is hard.

Guy Kawasaki

09
The Evidence-Based Funding Approach

The evidence-based funding approach is designed to fund founders – to help them progress with evidence of value. Not only does this work in the best interests of the founders in question, but potential investors too. In this approach, investors will significantly reduce the unnecessary risk of betting large sums on just big ideas and charming founders' pitch decks. Instead, they will empower accountable founders to explore and implement value in the real world. The approach allows investors to watch founders in action beyond the 15-minute pitch, while founders can get a fair chance to prove the potential of their startup value logic.

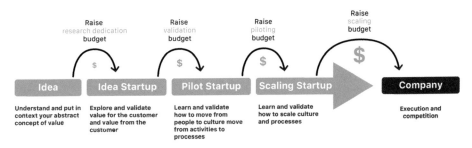

Figure 23: Funding Evidence-Based Progress

Ultimately, the approach will also allow investors to de-risk disruptive innovation-focused ventures early on. It is a win-win situation. Now, let's look at the level of funding required at inception.

At the beginning of their journey, founders will need a small budget that they can dedicate to early research. In other words, they need a small budget to dedicate the time and to access data, resources, and industry reports to conduct comprehensive similarity research. The time frame could be anything from a couple of weeks to a couple of months, and expected financial support can come from personal savings, family members, and friends. Upon completion of their research with a positive outcome, founders are capable of framing and articulating their idea into a value proposition for a specific customer within the context of market potential. At this point, the idea makes sense on paper.

Founders are now ready for the first of the Idea Startup Learning Maturity Level and should seek to raise a validation budget or enough money to conduct in-the-market experiments. They must do this to find enough evidence of the fact that the specific potential customers find value in what they're offering and are willing to pay money for it.

Instead of a pitch deck, they should present investors with the results of the conducted similarity research and a validation plan. In this validation plan, they should explain their approach to validate value for/from the customer within an agreed-upon time frame and a validation budget.

At the end of the Idea Startup Learning Maturity Level, founders pitch the evidence of value to potential angel investors and VC firms in order to raise the piloting budget.

Founders are now in the Piloting Startup Learning Maturity Level, and things are getting serious. This is when they should materialize value into a product/ service geared into a company that can produce it, sell it, and support it in a profitable and growing manner. In other words, founders will need enough funds to explore and build the infrastructure (culture + processes), hire their core team, and increase the fidelity of the product/service to the final customer version. But, most importantly, they will use the funding to test-run

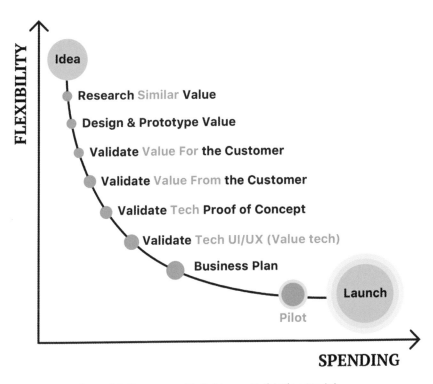

Figure 24: Progress with Evidence Validation Model

the business on a small scale and to prepare the company infrastructure for the scaling phase. At the end of this phase, founders will present the results of their piloting activities, product development achievements, and potential scaling plans to current as well as potential new investors. The founders have reached a point where everything is well set up and ready to go, like a rocket that is ready to launch. However, the proverbial rocket needs enough fuel to break through the stratosphere and reach space. At this point, they must decide on scaling benchmarks and the time frame required to achieve them with their investors. They are finally ready to launch the startup and begin scaling activities.

This approach allows accountable founders to progress with the highest flexibility possible while putting spending at the lowest possible point. In other words, it helps the founders and investors minimize risk.
Following this approach is especially great for founders who happen to be

innovating new value propositions and/or technologies. They can maximize their flexibility in making changes, updates, or even starting over with the least associated risks, including minimizing spending. It will keep founders focused on value and achieving evidence-based progress, all while being empowered by the investors' money.

So, how do we take the evidence-based approach?

Taking the Evidence-Based Funding Approach

To answer that question, let's start by asking another one. What do we get when the relationship between flexibility and spending is viewed from both the lens of the learning maturity levels and funding? We get an exciting, empowering relationship between a low-risk (maximum flexibility, minimum spending), value-focused startup journey, and clear investment milestones. The proposed approach creates a clear common language of value for founders and investors. It also outlines a clear path with even clearer milestones where investors and founders can measure startup progress based on real-world evidence beyond the hype and trendy concepts.

As founders progress on their startup journey, focusing only on learning without attaining tangible evidence to support those learnings can be counterproductive. Founders need to consider that potential investors will question everything that they are doing. Accordingly, progressing with evidence from one learning maturity level to another must be well documented and articulated.

Investors are encouraged to hire experienced coaches to accompany founders on their journey. The coaches will guide founders and serve as a second source of confirmation to the presented evidence at the end of every Learning Maturity Level. At this juncture, you can begin working on the following canvas as it will help you determine how much capital you need to start your venture.

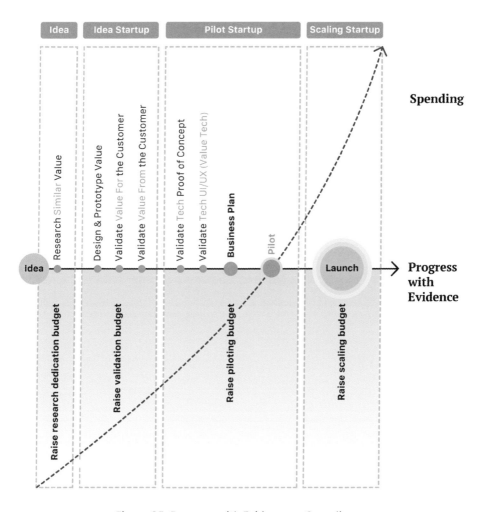

Figure 25: Progress with Evidence vs Spending

The Start! Capital Canvas

In the second phase of your startup journey – the idea startup – you answer the second question on the Value Exploration Stack regarding the potential of the value from the customer. The Start! Capital Canvas helps you to quickly evaluate The financial potential of your business model prototypes. Use this canvas to consider the different ways to maximize the profitability of your business model prototypes.

As mentioned, the purpose of this tool is to help you quickly estimate the potential revenues of your business model prototypes as well as the potential investment needed to start this business model.

Now, let's put it into practice.

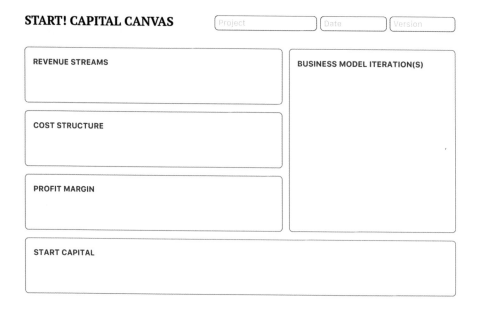

Figure 26: Start! Capital Canvas

How to use the tool

1 - Revenue Streams

- Understand the potential revenue streams: estimating sales volume and selling price per revenue stream. Together they make the total potential income per revenue stream. Potential revenue = selling price X sales volume.

2 - Cost Structure

- Understand the possible total costs including variable costs and fixed costs.

$$\textbf{Total Costs} = \textbf{Fixed Costs (FC) + Variable Costs (VC)}$$

3 - Profit Margin

- Estimate the projected profit of your business model prototypes.

$$\textbf{Profit} = \textbf{Total Revenue - Total Costs = (Selling Price x Sales Volume) - (FC +VC)}$$

- Estimate the projected profit margin.

$$\textbf{Profit Margin} = \textbf{((Selling Price x Sales Volume) - (FC + VC)) / (Selling Price x Sales Volume)}$$

- And your break-even point.

$$\textbf{Break-even point} = \text{FC / ((Sales Price) - (VC))}$$

4 - Business Model Iterations

- Once you have reached that point, you will need to think for a moment about whether or not the numbers feel good. Is the business model profitable? Are there ways that will allow the model to offer you better results? Can you make any modifications to your costs by outsourcing instead of operating your own production lines, for example?

  If the numbers don't feel good, consider making changes to the business model prototype. If, after making changes, the numbers are still looking unappealing, you can discard this business model prototype and move on to another one.

5 - START! Capital

- Up until this point, you will be figuring out the optimal operational costs and revenues of your business model prototype. If it has reached that point, it means that it has appealing revenues and positive profit margins. At this level, you have quickly estimated the OPEX[3] of your business model prototype.

  It is time to estimate how much initial capital is needed to acquire the key resources essential for materializing the key activities and the value proposition. Basically speaking, the CAPEX[4] of your business

---

3 Operating Expenses.
4 Capital Expenditure.

model. Figure out the key assets and resources that you will need to own and give it a ballpark number.

Now, add that number to the total amount of money you will need to cover the costs of your operations for at least the first 12 months of operations.

The resultant number is the amount of capital you will need to start your business.

When all is said and done, the startup journey involves transforming assumptions into tangible evidence. Meticulous documentation, singular ownership of experiments, uniform reporting, and a clear budget are crucial for successful experimentation. I can't stress the importance of validating critical assumptions enough. The evidence-based funding approach, aligned with value-focused and risk-mitigated progress fosters a low-risk, flexible startup journey with clear investment milestones.

3

The Braided Journey

"

Nothing is so awesomely unfamiliar as the familiar that discloses itself at the end of a journey.

Cynthia Ozick

10
The Braided Journey Of Entrepreneurship

You've made it to the final chapter on this journey and this is where the melding of the two arms of that journey begins to become more apparent. This is your introduction to what I call the Braided Journey of Entrepreneurship.

The uncertain journey of entrepreneurship is the path of transforming what is an abstract notion of value into what is tangible. It is the process of creating and materializing value in a profitable and scalable way under unforeseen conditions. Founders often don't seem to realize that the biggest challenges they will face on that journey happen unnoticeably on the mindset level first, only to become evident on the startup level later on. The mindset and the startup journeys are braided together, impacting and influencing each other.

The mindset journey is there to help you discover the vast universe of alternatives. If you rely only on the assumptions, experiments, and insights of the startup journey, it will keep you captured in a mental box of the limited options of what your perception is focused on. You need your mindset to continuously appreciate different perspectives to guide your experimentations and expand your understanding of what value could be.

On the other side, the startup journey is the materialization of your ideas and thoughts outside of the context of your mind and within the context of the world. It is the validation of what you perceive and the examination of what you think are your limitations. ***When combined together, both journeys are there to lead you from what you think you know to what is in reality actual.*** In a way, they both serve as each other's context. Without the mindset journey, the startup journey will be just a force without a direction. Without the startup journey, the mindset journey will just be an enveloped series of unfounded ideas and bucketloads of wishful thinking.

In this section of the book, we'll explore the impact and influence that both journeys can have on each other, using the perception presets as the main context of my exploration efforts.

THE BRAIDED JOURNEY

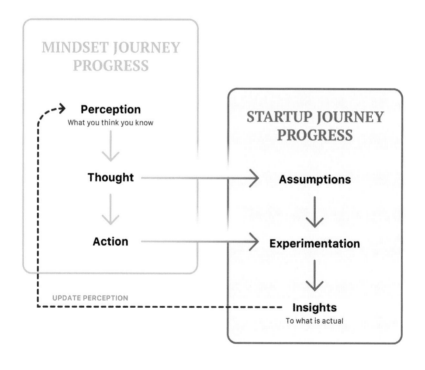

Figure 27: Braided Journey of Entrepreneurship

Perception Presets in the Braided Journey

How your mindset is already set up before you initiate the journey can make all the difference in how your journey can be shaped and defined. In that sense, the mindset journey becomes the point of reference on which the startup journey takes its guidance. Therefore, the mindset has the greatest influence on everything done on the startup journey.

In this section, I will describe the connection and impact of the mindset and the startup journey on how you make progress within your entrepreneurial adventure. The mindset presets will be used as a starting point. Both the mindset and startup journey are very dynamic in how they interact and contribute to each other. The three types of presets mentioned earlier are the most commonly observed in the field.

A quick reminder that the three types of mindset presets are:

1. Based on what entrepreneurs *know*, they go forward and *implement their ideas*.

2. Based on what entrepreneurs *think they know*, they seek what they think they *should know*.

3. Based on what entrepreneurs *think they know*, they seek what they think they *don't know*.

Type 1

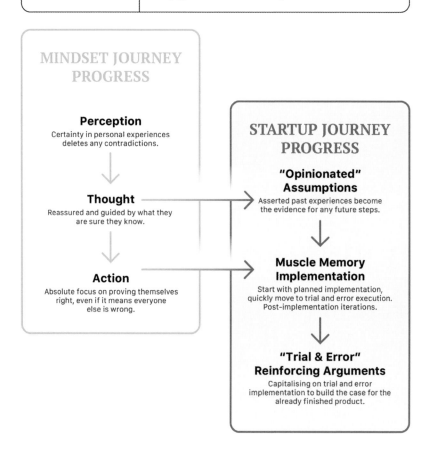

Figure 28: Braided Journey - Type 1

Type 1 founders go through a very interesting braided journey of entrepreneurship. It is a never-ending battle to force what is perceived on what is real. No matter what evidence reality might manifest throughout the journey, Type 1 founders seem to find a way to manipulate arguments to favor their own points of view.

They force it, sometimes without even attempting to hide it. Not only do they force it in front of the people around them, but also to themselves. It is a sign of absolute assurance in what they know. And they should feel that way. After all, most of them are highly skilled professionals and have a lot of experience in the world.

However, what they really fail to grasp is that all of that experience and skill becomes a limitation to their perception, used mainly to keep it boxed comfortably within the walls of familiar knowledge.

Type 1 founders are very keen on success. To attain it, they are willing to do anything, including sacrificing their own perception of reality. They work diligently to manifest their vision of the "perfect product".

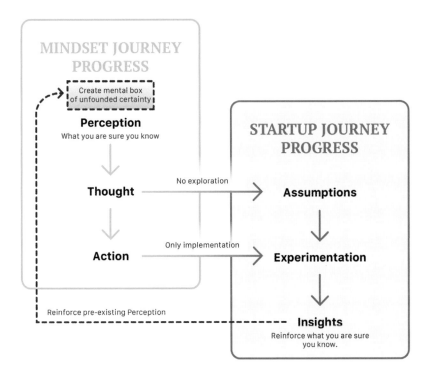

Figure 29: Feedback Loop in Type 1

An overconfident founder perception promotes reassured thoughts and opinionated assumptions about the product. The founder is adamant that their previous professional experiences are the best evidence for any future steps. Thus, those reassured thoughts translate into an absolutely focused "I am right" action and it manifests into a full-speed-ahead, well-planned implementation document. Later on, that document is completely ignored and replaced with a trial-and-error kind of execution, coupled with many halfway and unthoughtful product iterations.

Finally, the founder reaches a point where they will capitalize on the trial-and-error results to build the case for the already-built product. When this process becomes repetitive, it reinforces the pre-existing perceptions and solidifies the walls of the mental box of unfounded certainty. The Type 1 Braided Journey thus becomes a loop created to trap founders inside a very unrealistic, yet very comfortable, mental box of unfounded certainty.

In the winter of 2022, during a mentoring event organized by a local incubator, I met with an engineer who was building a tech-based startup. He started the conversation by complaining about investors and how they are not putting money into his startup. He referred to his time at a multinational organization where he worked as an engineering project manager and how his superiors (comparing managers to investors in this instance) listened and supported his initiatives as well as his ideas at work in a far better way. As we continued our conversation (me listening, and him talking, in this case), he was keen to showcase how much his background helped him overcome the many hurdles he faced in building the technology and almost creating the final prototypes. What was missing was finding some components and his proof of concept would be complete.

"If only investors would see my vision for the technology," he said.

So, I asked him: "And what is your vision for the technology?"

For the next thirty minutes, I listened to an unstoppable abstract monologue about the potential of technology and how, when produced locally, it could make all the difference for the future. So, I asked him if the technology he was building was similar to an already-available tech. He confirmed it and stressed that he was trying to build the same technology locally.

"And how can you use this technology to help customers? And in what context?" I asked.

He explained that the technology could be used in multiple ways and for different customers. He then went back to talk about his time at a multi-national company and how he managed to overcome challenges, obstacles, and a lack of vision. He referred to what he was experiencing with his startup as a similar situation and that it was only a matter of time until he prevailed. He reiterated that this was the cost he had to pay for his dreams to come true.

The founder had spent time, effort, and money working on building a technology that was already available on the market, without having a specific final product for a specific customer in mind. He was being refused by investors because he kept selling them a technology that already existed while asking for funds to buy components to finish his proof of concept. Investors generally don't offer research and development (R&D) grants, they offer investments in potentially profitable businesses.

The founder had ignored plenty of the hints from interactions and events. Yes, he had put a lot of effort into his work and, I must admit, a lot of passion too. But he was too confident in his capabilities to accept rejection. So much so that he kept pushing forward despite the obvious. I could clearly see how exhausted he was, both mentally and physically. But he was not ready to quit yet.

I shared all of that with him – with as much compassion and pleasantness as I could, and he wasn't very happy with what I had to say. As our session time was nearing an end, I shared some ideas on how to focus his thoughts around value and how to progress with value. He kept silent and didn't show interest in what I was saying. When the time was up, he thanked me and left.

In the winter of 2019, I was at a startup retreat with a local accelerator. On the second day, I woke up early and went outside to enjoy a bit of nature. I was sitting at a big lake surrounded by beautiful desert sand on one side, and gorgeous green farmland on the other side. The sun was shining and the air was crisp. I remember it very well because it was the last time I saw the beauty of nature like this before the COVID-19 lockdowns began in Egypt.

As I was staring at the peaceful view, I heard someone calling my name calmly. I turned and I found a polite gentleman looking at me. He was one of the founders on the retreat and he was wondering if we could have a chat about his startup. He was working on a really great technology, building a breakthrough solution, and explained how much his solution made all the difference to his clients. However, he was facing challenges with his customers' demands. He believed strongly in the applications of the technology and he undertook many projects with diverse and very different applications of the tech just to make a point. As he continued his story, he also explained how his business background had served his startup journey well and how much he learned from his previous successes and failures. He shared a wonderful vision of the future using his technology and was incredibly passionate about it. He gave multiple examples of how his technology could have many applications in several very different industries and how it could change the everyday life of his customers.

Despite all his passion, his background as a serial entrepreneur along with his big-name client list and the amazing tech videos he showed me on his phone, he never showed me a final product or service. Nor did he show me a tangible market strategy. As the conversation went on, he kept pointing to all the possibilities the tech could achieve for Business to Business (B2B), Business to Customers (B2C), and Business to Business to Customers (B2B2C) customers.

As the exchange continued, I started to see an underfunded company with a non-patentable technology and many possible market applications but no clear business model.

"To accomplish your vision, you need to start somewhere," I said to him. "Perhaps, you should consider focusing on only one of your tech's possible applications. The one with the highest possible sales potential in terms of volume or price, or both. That might help you build up your company infrastructure, hire skilled team members, build up your brand, and, most importantly, create reliable revenue streams. Attacking on all fronts with the very limited resources you have will kill the company's chances of survival. Trying to push the technology to different customer segments in different industries, with a very small team, is not a sound strategy. Every new project you take will get you in deeper trouble."

He was not very happy with my answer. He thought that I was limiting the potential of his company and couldn't see the bigger picture. He started talking about his vision and how much he had sacrificed, personally and professionally, to see it happen.

I met with him often after that and, every time, his opinion and point of view stood in the way of any insight he personally collected from the field. His fascination with the technology and what it could do had, somehow, blinded him from considering the well-being of the startup, not to mention his own personal well-being.

All of the examples he shared with me for existing customers pointed to the fact that he had built a software/ hardware, project-based contracting company that offered customized solutions to other businesses. However, he was pitching the company as a tech startup with a unique final product that could easily be reproduced and sold at scale. The first kind of startup needed a huge focus on cash flow and on pursuing projects with high customization components. This business model required a strong sales team with good connections in the ready- to-sell-to industries.

But the second kind he was pitching was a company that focused on marketing an easy-to-use, tech-based product that needed to be available in as many online/offline distribution channels as possible. This business model needed to produce and sell at a growing rate to achieve profitability. It also needed a low touch but direct customer relationship.

These were two completely different business models with absolutely different needs as well as capital to operate and start. He could not do both at the same time with the limited resources and capabilities he had at the time. He must start with one and move forward with the second when it is strategically wise to do so.

I must admit that this founder is unique in terms of determination and his willingness to achieve a wonderful vision. ***But any vision must be actionable and must start somewhere.***

Type 2

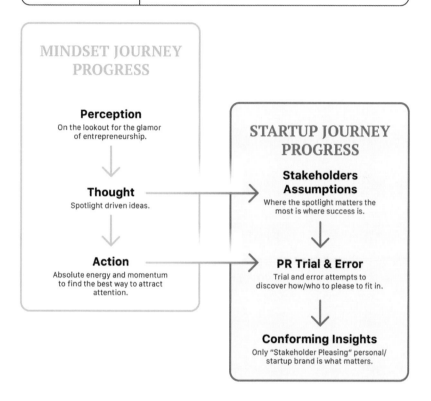

Figure 30: Braided Journey - Type 2

The Type 2 Founders Braided Journey is the pilgrimage to the limelight. Founders focus on their personal branding more than on the startup itself. In this case, the startup becomes a necessary accessory to accomplish that target. After all, one cannot become a rock star founder without a glamorous startup!

Type 2 founders begin with a perception well-marinated in the glamorous potential of entrepreneurship. Accordingly, Type 2 founders' perception definition of success through entrepreneurship is equivalent to a personal brand completely submerged in the limelight and a part of the chosen few: being chosen to join the cohort of a famous incubator in California, being chosen to receive funding from a well renowned global venture capital fund, or being featured as a key speaker in a must- go-to event in Silicon Valley or maybe Alexandria. They have plenty of spotlight ideas and thoughts that grow exponentially and dominate their imagination.

Those ideas and thoughts become so intense that the founders can almost taste the limelight and touch the social media posts likes and shares. They become a forceful source of inspiration, accelerating the founders' momentum in "seeking the spotlight to succeed" tremendously. The founders become obsessed with how to attract attention and keep the focus solely on their own personal brand. That of course includes building a startup with some of the most interesting buzzwords filled with claims, told with passionate storytelling, and mostly forced arguments. Needless to say, nothing will stop them from living their own definition of success.

Under the influence of the glamor-filled thoughts of success, the founders build assumption-based criteria for what they deem the most useful stakeholder traits and attractive qualities that can be most helpful in reaching their goals. They quickly follow that with a fierce trial-and-error approach of who would best fit that criteria and what to do to be chosen by those identified stakeholders. Usually, those founders go for well-funded programs with brand names that are well-recognized by the community. After all, adding that logo to the pitch deck must add value. It isn't important to be chosen by a brand that isn't recognized for its excellence or isn't appreciated by the surrounding community.

As the founders continue their battle for the spotlight and personal gratification, they keep discovering new insights about how to conform better, be chosen faster, and be part of the elite of the community.

Those are the founders you always hear about, but hear almost nothing about their startups. They accomplish much on the frontiers of PR and personal branding, but their startups are just a name on LinkedIn that comes right before the word CEO or Founder.

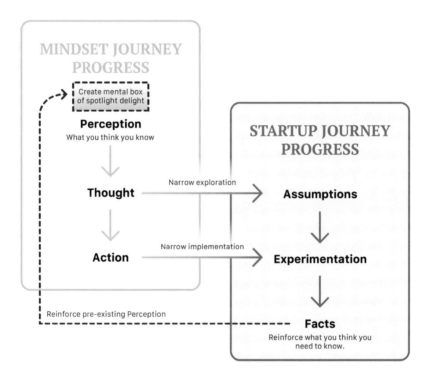

Figure 31: Feedback Loop in Type 2

The Braided Journey for Type 2 founders becomes an infinite loop, nurtured to build this mental box of spotlight delight. It is characterized by narrow exploration and implementation, focused mostly on feeding the ego of the founders with limelight delights rather than their pockets with profits and their mindsets with knowledge.

In the summer of 2016, I met a really ambitious and smart young founder during a training program with a local support program. The founder reached out to me after the program, looking for mentoring sessions. During our first session, we had a conversation about her startup and why she started it.

What do you aim to achieve, I asked her.

"I want to become like [the name of a well-known founder]", she answered quickly, assertively, and passionately.

"But why become like this 'well-known' person?"

"Because he is well connected and well respected", she responded.

"And how will you accomplish that?"

"I am not sure yet, but I think I am on the right track."

At that moment, I understood that we would not talk about the startup.

"Ok, then describe what you mean by the right track," I said.

She looked at me with her piercing eyes and started telling me about how she already won a regional competition with her startup and how she was applying to bigger competitions in the fall. All she needed was to develop a great pitch deck, to convince the panel, and to win. Then, she started to take my opinion about the logo of the company and showed me different designs, colors, and patterns. It was very interesting to see the number of details discussed with a large amount of buzzwords.

"I wish you would put half of this effort into your business model," I said.

"But the investors don't care about the business model. They want the buzz and this happens by winning competitions with a large following online and by becoming the founder they never could be."

"So, you think the investors wouldn't care that you don't have a clear value proposition with a sustainable revenue stream?"

"Yes, I do," she said in a challenging and confident manner. "I am a female founder, I have a large following online, my startup has great social impact, and I look great in front of the camera. Their investment in me would buy them a lot of goodwill with their limited partners (LP)."

For those who are not familiar with the term, a limited partner (LP) is the provider of capital for venture funds to make investments.

"So why you are here?"

"I wanted to ask you if I can put you on the pitch deck as my mentor. Would that be ok with you?"

"If that can help you, of course. However, in return, I need you to spend time working on your value proposition and revenue stream. That is my only request. Would that be ok with you?"

She promised me that she would make the effort.

I never saw her again!

If you are wondering what happened to this young lady, I want to share with you that she is now well accomplished and successful, and her startup took her places far beyond the 'well- known founder', by whom she was so inspired.

Type 3

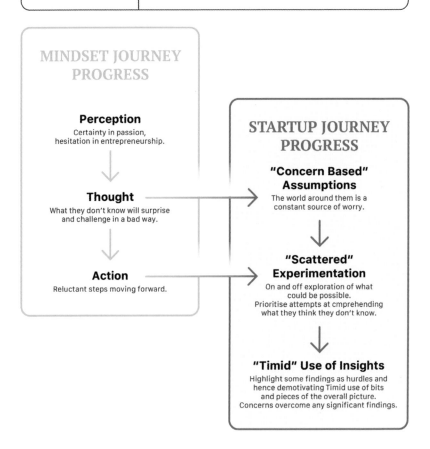

Figure 32: Braided Journey - Type 3

Type 3 founders experience "the rollercoaster" braided journey. It is full of frequent passion-fueled "ups", combined with plenty of doubt-induced "downs". Many people can mistake Type 3 founders for the typical fearful or scared entrepreneurs, but they couldn't be more wrong. Type 3 founders care so much about what they are building that it can render them timid in implementation. They are protecting the purity of their dream from the red tape and the pragmatic cynicism of the world. They worry too much, especially about all the things they think they should absolutely be an expert on which they later discover they don't. Many of them spend a lot of time worrying about taxes, accounting, paperwork, and all the things in between. It consumes their energy and drains their passion.

Passionate founders are also often very imaginative and, from my interactions with them in the field, many of them seem to get obsessed with their imagination instead of with their passion and how they can materialize it. A simple example would be the *founders spending a lot of time thinking about the potential of their ideas and doing too little to make it happen. They keep pondering the details and the possible versions of their ideas, and even consider how some might react to them.*

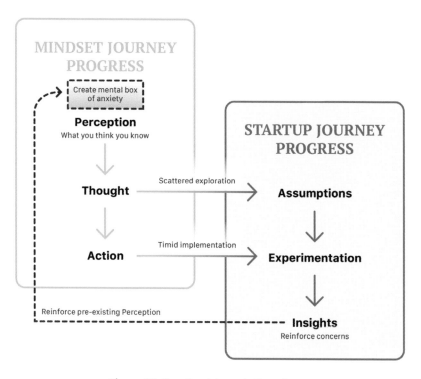

Figure 33: Feedback Loop in Type 3

Another common example falls a little on the darker side of things. It happens when founders become obsessed with a negative line of imagination. In other words, they ponder all of the things that could potentially go wrong with their ideas and then they get obsessed with them. Sometimes, they obsess to the extent that they are rendered immobile. They stand still – torn between imagination and passion in such a way that, in some cases, can cause real suffering.

In the fall of 2022, a dear friend recommended that I speak with a founder of a social enterprise. She described him as one of the most passionate entrepreneurs she had ever met. Naturally, I was drawn to meeting him. My friend would not describe anyone as the most passionate unless he had made a really big impression on her. So, we scheduled a phone call and had a chat. I asked the founder to share his challenges. He was building a social enterprise that was focused on creating real impact.

The passion was really clear in all the stories he shared, describing the beneficiaries and using terms of affection and endearment. It was as if he were talking about his very own children. He really cared and sincerely wanted to make a difference. But, for some reason, it didn't seem like he was making much progress on his journey.

So I asked him, "I feel that something is stopping you or at least slowing you down from making real progress. Can you share with me a bit more?"

"I don't want my startup to lose value."

"I don't get what you mean. Can you elaborate a bit more?"

"I sense that I will have to compromise on the value I am offering just to be funding worthy. I am also concerned about the infinite number of rules I have to follow in order to be able to do business legitimately. I am afraid I will need an army of lawyers and accountants just to register the company, not to mention a ton of money to pay for all that. It is like I am trying to push a mountain on a slippery upward slope."

He paused for a moment and continued, "I spend hours reading the laws and the regulations, trying to interpret which ones are best for me as a social enterprise. The times that I've discussed this with many lawyers and accountants, I've rarely found clear answers. I am really concerned about starting on the wrong foot and not being able to get this organization together correctly from day one."

Watching the conversation going into the anxious realm of "what could go wrong" imagining, I asked the founder to share his progress on the business model, specifically on the revenue stream part of it. He paused and said, "I will send you something later today."

That night, I received a really large Word document with charts, tables, numbers, and possible go-to-market plans.

When I asked him why he was not moving forward with any of these well-researched plans, he told me: "I don't want to lose everything that I want to build just because I wasn't really ready."

This founder was clearly wrapped up in the darker side of his imagination. He cared so much about the people whom his startup would serve that he didn't want to launch prematurely. However, this can – sometimes – be just as detrimental as launching without prior research. After some time, he eventually launched the startup and, to this day, he is passionately creating impact. However, he is struggling with achieving real progress.

As you can see, the braided journey highlights how the presets within the startup journey as well as the mindset journey – if not addressed correctly at each stage – can be detrimental to a founder's overall journey. ***At this point, you can complete your final exercise. That's up next.***

"I Am Grateful For..." Exercise

Now that you've reached the end of your journey, it's time to reflect.
I learned this exercise from one of my mentees. She is one of the hardest working entrepreneurs I had the pleasure to meet on my journey as a mentor.

Putting it into practice

Setting Choose a quiet place .

Tools Pen, paper, and your favorite beverage (and maybe cookies).

Type Personal exercise.

When During a setback to your startup.

Exercise Steps:

1. Write down everything/everyone you are grateful to have in your life.

2. Organize them in order of importance to you.

3. Write down your thoughts for each and keep them handy. Every time you feel low or down, look at your list and remind yourself that you have so much in your life.

4. Do something to show your gratitude. If you are grateful to have a certain person in your life, tell them. If you are grateful for your health, take better care of it. Commit to it, it will make all the difference.

Once you finish it, hang it where you can see it often, like on your bathroom mirror. ***It is a helpful reminder.***

Final Thoughts Of Goodwill & Respect

At this point, take a minute to offer yourself a massive congratulations for reaching the end of this guide. I'm almost certain that a large number of you were faced with a few uncomfortable truths and that couldn't have been easy for you. However, if you're serious about your entrepreneurial journey, I implore you to not take anything personally. Instead, look at your startup from the perspective of an objective outsider.

For my fellow mentors who will read this book, use this as your foundation, upon which you build your mentoring efforts. The reflections and insights that will come from your mentoring will provide growth and development not only for your mentees but for you as well.

For me, writing this book has been a journey of reflection and it all started with the question I asked myself on the day I celebrated a decade of working and contributing to the Egyptian startup ecosystem. The question was: What have you learned from working with founders in the past ten years?

The answer I reached that day was the nucleus upon which I wrote this book.

Building a startup is more about learning than about glamour or funding. The first is the focus of the journey while the second and third are potential results of that journey of learning. In the context of entrepreneurship, learning and the implementation of those learnings create progress.

The conscious decision to venture on a startup adventure sparks a subconscious decision to embark on a mindset journey. The two journeys are distinctive and give context to each other. They both have two unique systems of progress.

The mindset journey system's progress begins with perception. Based on how the founder perceives the world, feelings and thoughts are created. Eventually, they are translated into actions.

The startup journey system of progress begins with a founder's assumptions about the business. They are tested with experiments with the purpose of gaining insights.

Together, both systems of progress give each other direction and purpose. They allow founders the opportunity to expand from what they know to what is real and actual. Connecting both systems of progress allows the perception to stay unboxed from the high walls that personal experience and assumptions can build around the mindset. The connection offers the opportunity to interpret experiment-based insights from the potential of different perspectives, hence, expanding the conversation from what we know to what is actual and factual in the real world. When this loop is concisely mastered by founders, they will be able to make progress on their journey of entrepreneurship without letting one side dominate the other. Making sure that both sides are balanced, feeding each other with enough information to make the next step on the journey, is crucial.

This book journey reminded me of the many untold battles of Egyptian founders. Reliving some of those experiences with the purpose of understanding and appreciating them hasn't been easy. As a mentor, one of the hardest moments on my journey was witnessing the unseen but expensive human cost of entrepreneurship.

Despite my best efforts, I wasn't always capable of helping everyone that life has sent my way.

Nothing I can write will ever really describe what these brave souls go through to build their companies, their careers, and lives. I have been there when founders lost their companies, lost their teams, lost loved ones, suffered mental breakdowns, and, in some cases, lost everything they had worked very hard to accomplish. I witnessed determination in standing up to blunt rejection. I saw the passion of one person igniting the hearts of teams with the will to fight at the darkest of moments. I encountered faith when it was not possible and watched creative minds turn nothing into stardust. I witnessed female founders stand up to stereotyping and prejudice with unhinging firmness of purpose. I marveled at the grace often displayed in the face of defeat, the kindness of the few countering the aggression of the many, and the shy but absolute happiness exhibited when a milestone was successfully accomplished.

But perhaps the most unbelievable thing I observed was villains becoming saints and saints transforming into villains. This is perhaps the most eyebrow-raising of them all.

So, to my dear founders, I am grateful for everything I have learned from you during this decade-long journey. Being a part of your journey has been the greatest privilege of my life.

In this book, I shared with you almost everything I learned during my journey as a mentor and it is my sincerest hope that it will spark the resolve in you that you need to push ahead.

Goodwill and respect.

Hani W. Naguib

About The Author

A mentor and a dedicated advocate for fostering innovation, Hani W. Naguib has woven together a deep understanding of entrepreneurship with a passion for empowering founders. With a wealth of experience, Naguib has played a pivotal role in advising numerous local program teams, imparting invaluable insights into the development of founder-centric programs.

In collaboration with leading programs across Egypt, Africa, and Europe, Naguib has been instrumental in creating immersive learning experiences that empower aspiring entrepreneurs with the tools and knowledge needed to navigate the complexities of the startup landscape. To influence positive change, he has volunteered more than 10,000 hours to support early-stage founders to begin their journey on the right track. He has also offered free mentoring sessions for idea-phase and early-stage startup founders — 70% of which are dedicated to founders who are not affiliated with formal support programs.

With a commitment to fostering innovation and a track record of influencing positive change with entrepreneurship, Naguib has been presented with the prestigious African Ecosystem Hero of the Year Award, 2023 by Global Startup Awards. As he continues to make contributions to the entrepreneurial ecosystem, he remains dedicated to shaping the next generation of visionary leaders and fostering a culture of innovation worldwide.

ACKNOWLEDGMENTS

I am sincerely grateful for

My Parents. All the love.
Thank you

Dr. Amr Shaarawi for inspiring my journey and his contagious kind spirit.
Thank you

Dr. Mohamed Mohamady for his non-stop encouragement and positive faith.
Thank you

Ahmed Abdel Hamid for his friendship and genuine support on this journey.
Thank you

Melissa Mitchell for her sincere advice and her committed spirit to make my writing and this book better.
Thank you

The American University in Cairo Venture Lab team for their valuable and positive spirit along my journey.
Thank you

Early Readers

(in alphabetical order)
I am eternally grateful that you took the time to read and offer your very valuable input. Your comments resonated as I was writing and updating the text. Thank you.

Dr. Ayman Ismail

Fatima El Saadany

Hazem El Wessimy

Hazem Yones

Magda Elsehrawi

Tarek Seif El Nasr

Last but not least

I would like to thank all the founders who allowed me to take part in their journey and witness the true magnitude of the human spirit.

Important to highlight

The book draws on my experiences with 1000+ founders in the past decade. Here I am highlighting 90 startups that contributed vividly to the examples in the book.

Glossary of Terms

Actionable Vision Canvas
A canvas designed to connect an entrepreneur's personal mindset progress with the startup's progress. It helps communicate and align the vision with co-founders.

Braided Journey of Entrepreneurship
The interconnected and intertwined nature of the mindset journey and the startup journey in entrepreneurship, highlighting how progress in one influences the other.

Balancing Act
Metaphor for the precarious nature of entrepreneurship, requiring the ability to balance multiple factors, make decisions under pressure, and navigate uncertainties.

Business Model
The way a company creates, delivers, and captures value. It includes elements like revenue streams, customer segments, channels, and cost structures.

Capital Expenditure (CAPEX)
The estimated initial capital required to acquire key resources essential for materializing key activities and the value proposition in a business model prototype.

Curiosity
Inquisitive nature, the desire to ask questions, explore possibilities, and seek innovative solutions, an inherent quality in entrepreneurs.

Customer Validation
The process of confirming that a product or service addresses the needs of the target market through direct interaction and feedback from potential customers.

Discipline in Entrepreneurship
The ability of an entrepreneur to adhere to a structured and focused approach, emphasizing consistency, persistence, and dedication.

Dreaming
The underrated quality of envisioning possibilities and motivating oneself to learn, persevere, and overcome

challenges in the entrepreneurial journey.

Entrepreneur Journey Map Kit
A set of tools and exercises designed to help entrepreneurs navigate and understand their mindset journey. Includes the Entrepreneur Journey Map (EMJ), Actionable Vision Canvas, and Team Mission Canvas.

Entrepreneurship
The spirit of asking questions, imagining, creating, and taking risks; a journey of making progress, learning by doing, and creating value.

Evidence-Based Funding Approach
An approach designed to fund founders based on evidence of value, reducing the risk for investors by allowing them to observe founders in action beyond pitch decks and providing innovating founders with a fair chance to prove their startup's potential.

Feedback Loop
A recurring cycle of thoughts and actions that reinforce certain behaviors. In Type 1, it involves an overconfident founder promoting reassured thoughts and opinions, leading to a loop of unfounded certainty. In Type 2, it revolves around building a mental box of spotlight delight, with a narrow focus on personal branding. In Type 3, it encompasses worry and imagination loops that can hinder progress.

Growth-Hacking
The use of creative and unconventional strategies to rapidly grow a startup, often involving a combination of marketing, product development, and data analytics.

High-Wire Act
An analogy for entrepreneurship, symbolizing the risky and challenging journey of making progress despite limited resources and uncertainty.

Idea Startup Learning Maturity Level
The early phase of the startup journey where founders transform assumptions into hypotheses and validate them through experiments to gather evidence of value before seeking significant funding.

Independence in Entrepreneurship	The preference or desire of an entrepreneur to operate and lead a business without relying on a co-founder, often associated with autonomy and decision-making control.
Informed Optimism	The third phase of the Entrepreneur Mindset Journey, characterized by a deep understanding of the journey, appreciation for its effects, and a faster progress towards goals.
Lean Methodology	An approach to startup development that emphasizes iterative product releases, rapid prototyping, and continuous validation based on customer feedback.
Learning Maturity Levels	Different stages in the startup journey, categorized by assumptions, experiments, and insights. Each level involves progressing from business-related assumptions to mature insights through experimentation.
Limelight Delight	A term associated with Type 2 founders, describing their focus on attracting attention and achieving personal gratification through public recognition rather than tangible business success.
Mentorship	The guidance and support provided by experienced individuals to entrepreneurs, helping them navigate challenges, make informed decisions, and progress on their journey.
Mindset Journey	The internal development and psychological aspects of an entrepreneur, encompassing attitudes, beliefs, and perspectives that influence decision-making.
Mindset Journey Kit	A set of tools and exercises designed to help entrepreneurs navigate and understand their mindset journey. Includes the Entrepreneur Journey Map (EMJ), Actionable Vision Canvas, and Team Mission Canvas.
Mindset System of Progress	A structured approach to developing and evolving the mindset of an entrepreneur, emphasizing perception, thought, action..

Outcome vs. Output Distinguishing between the tangible results (output) and the real impact or value created (outcome) in entrepreneurial endeavors.

Organic Growth The natural and gradual expansion of a business without relying heavily on external funding, often driven by increasing sales and customer acquisition.

Perception Presets Different types of mindset presets influencing the entrepreneurial journey:

> **Type 1:** Founders proceed based on what they know, often leading to an overconfident approach that may hinder adaptability and learning.

> **Type 2:** Founders focus on personal branding and seeking the spotlight, emphasizing public recognition over business fundamentals.

> **Type 3:** Founders experience a rollercoaster journey with passion-fueled "ups" and doubt-induced "downs," sometimes becoming immobilized by concerns.

Pitch Deck A presentation that provides an overview of a startup's business plan, typically used to attract investors or partners.

Problem-Solution Fit The phase in entrepreneurship where entrepreneurs identify and validate the problem they aim to solve before creating a solution.

Product-Market Fit The stage in a startup's development where the product meets the needs and demands of the target market, indicating a match between the product and the market.

Psychological Component in Entrepreneurship The influence of psychological factors on the decision-making and behavior of entrepreneurs, particularly in the context of rushing into product launches without adequate groundwork.

Research Grant   Funding provided to researchers or entrepreneurs for conducting research, often associated with academic or scientific endeavors.

Resilience   The ability to bounce back from setbacks, failures, or challenges, a crucial skill for entrepreneurs to persevere in the face of uncertainties.

Revenue Stream   The source of income for a business, detailing how it earns money through the sale of products, services, or other means.

Social Enterprise   An organization that applies commercial strategies to maximize improvements in financial, social, and environmental well-being. It focuses on creating positive social impact while sustaining itself financially.

Solo Founder   An entrepreneur who starts and operates a business independently without a co-founder or business partner. Also referred to as a solopreneur or sole proprietor.

Startup Journey   The external journey of creating and developing a business, involving ideation, product development, market entry, and scaling.

Startup System of Progress   A structured approach to progressing through the stages of a startup, including idea validation, product development, market entry, and growth.

Start! Capital Canvas   A tool used in the idea startup phase to estimate potential revenues, total costs, profit margins, and break-even points for business model prototypes, aiding founders in evaluating the financial viability of their startup.

Team Mission Canvas   A canvas focusing on aligning the startup's big picture with the team's mindset. It compiles objectives from the Actionable Vision Canvas into an executable mission.

Testing Activities   Entrepreneurial activities conducted to learn about the functionality and reliability of the technology needed to materialize a value proposition, ranging from proof of concept development to creating a final product.

Uncertain Journey of Entrepreneurship
The challenging and unpredictable path that entrepreneurs navigate, involving both the mindset and startup journeys, characterized by learning, adaptation, and progress.

Validation
The process of confirming the viability, feasibility, and desirability of a business idea, product, or solution through evidence and feedback.

Value Creation
The process of adding value to products, services, or solutions, a fundamental goal in entrepreneurship.

Value Exploration Stack
A toolkit for entrepreneurs during the idea startup learning phase, emphasizing an iterative approach to understanding value through four main questions related to customer benefits, business benefits, technical proof of concept, and user experience.

Value-Focused Venture
A business or entrepreneurial endeavor centered on creating value for customers, solving problems, and making a positive impact.

Waterfall Approach
A traditional project management approach where progress flows in one direction through a sequence of phases, often contrasted with agile or iterative methodologies.

List Of Tables & Figures

✳ The author is the source of all figures in the book. Copyrights are reserved.

References &
Citations

1. Zemeckis, Robert (Director).(2015). The walk (Film). Tri-Star Pictures.

2. Kelly, D., and Connor, D. R. (1979). The emotional cycle of change. The 1979 Annual Handbook for Group Facilitators.

3. Kambourova, Z., & Stam, F.C. (2016). Entrepreneurs' Overoptimism During The Early Life Course Of The Firm.

4. Pulford, B. D., & Colman, A. M. (1996). Overconfidence, base rates and outcome positivity/ negativity of predicted events. British Journal of Psychology, 87(3), 431–445. https://doi.org/ 10.1111/j.2044-8295.1996.tb02600.x

5. Hmieleski, K. M., & Baron, R. A. (2009). Entrepreneurs' optimism and new venture performance: A social cognitive perspective. Academy of Management Journal, 52(3), 473–488. https://doi.org/10.5465/AMJ.2009.41330755

6. Sanchez, C., & Dunning, D. (2018). Overconfidence among beginners: Is a little learning a dangerous thing? Journal of Personality and Social Psychology, 114(1), 10–28. https:// doi. org/10.1037/pspa0000102

7. Blank S. The four steps to the epiphany: successful strategies for products that win. Foster City (CA): Cafepress; 2005. pp. 17-28.

8. EU-Startups. Samuel Villegas. July 18, 2019. The startup grind: why starting a business is stressful and can even be depressing. www.eu-startups.com/2019/07/the-startup-grind-why-starting-a-business-is-stressful-and-can-even-be-depressing

9. Cope, Jason. (2011). Entrepreneurial Learning from Failure: An Interpretative Phenomenological Analysis. Journal of Business Venturing. 26. 604-623. DOI:10.1016/j. jbusvent.2010.06.002

10. Clore, Gerald & Huntsinger, Jeffrey. (2007). How Emotions Inform Judgment and Regulate Thought. Trends in cognitive sciences. 11. 393-9. DOI: 10.1016/j.tics.2007.08.005.

11. Arenius, Pia & Minniti, Maria. (2005). Perceptual Variables and Nascent Entrepreneurship. Small Business Economics. 24. 233-247. 10.1007/s11187-005-1984-x.

12. Elliot, A.J. (1997). Integrating 'classic' and 'contemporary' approaches to achievement motivation: a hierarchical model of approach and avoidance achievement motivation. In Pintrich, P. and Maehr, M. (eds), Advances in Motivation and Achievement. Greenwich, CT: JAI Press, pp. 143–179.

13. Barnes et al. Creating & delivering your value proposition managing customer experience for profit. London and Philadelphia. Kogan Page Limited. pp.28.

14. Christensen, Clayton M., Taddy Hall, Karen Dillon, and David S. Duncan. "Know Your Customers' 'Jobs to Be Done'." Harvard Business Review 94, no. 9 (September 2016): 54–62.

15. Forbes. Kaan Turnali. March 20, 2016. The Art And Science Of Customer Empathy In Design Thinking. www.forbes.com/sites/ sap/2016/03/20/the-art-and-science-of-customer-empathy-in- design-thinking

16. Tuckman, B., 1965. Developmental sequence in small groups. Psychological Bulletin, 63(6), pp. 384-399.

17. Bloomberg Business Week. Olivia Zaleski, Peter Waldman and Ellen Huet. September 22, 2016. How Hampton-Creek sold Silicon Valley on a fake-Mayo miracle. www.bloomberg.com/ features/2016-hampton-creek-just-mayo

18. CB Insights. CB Insights Editors. May 23, 2019. 16 Of The Biggest Alleged Startup Frauds Of All Time. www.cbinsights.com/research/biggest-startup-frauds

19. Business Insider. Kevin Loria. October 15, 2015. This isn't the first time people have raised troubling questions about Theranos. www.businessinsider.com/science-of-elizabeth-holmes-theranos-update-2015-4

20. Tech Crunch. Ron Miller. September 10, 2022. How Zoho became a $1B company without a dime of external investment. www.techcrunch.com/2022/09/10/how-zoho-became-1b-company-without-a-dime-of-external-investment

21. The Guardian. Benjamin Lee. October 21, 2020. Quibi: shortform streaming service to shut down after six months. www.theguardian.com/culture/2020/oct/21/quibi-shut-down-jeffrey-katzenberg-meg-whitman

22. Britanica. The Editors of Encyclopedia Britannica. Jeffrey Katzenberg. www.britannica.com/biography/Jeffrey- Katzenberg

23. Forbes. The Forbes Editorial Team. Profile - Meg Whitman. www.forbes.com/profile/meg-whitman/?sh=2219915a63cc

24. Harvard Business Review. Steve Blank. August 20, 2018. NewTV Is the Antithesis of a Lean Startup. Can It Work? www.hbr.org/ 2018/08/newtv-is-the-antithesis-of-a-lean-startup-can-it- work

25. Tech Crunch. Lucas Matney. July 8, 2020. Report says Quibi lost 92% of its earliest users after free trials expired. www.techcrunch.com/2020/07/08/report-says-quibi-lost-92- of-its-earliest-users-after-free-trials-expired

26. The Information. Tom Dotan, Jessica Toonkel. October 21, 2020. The Investors Who Face Big Losses From the Quibi Collapse. www.theinformation.com/articles/the-investors- who-face-big-losses-from-the-quibi-collapse